Memoirs of the Civil War

T0163255

Captain William W. Chamberlaine in 1863.

Seeing the Elephant: Southern Eyewitnesses to the Civil War

Series Editors
Gary Gallagher
Robert K. Krick

Memoirs of the Civil War

Between the Northern and Southern
Sections of the United States of America
1861 to 1865

CAPTAIN WILLIAM W. CHAMBERLAINE
OF THE CONFEDERATE STATES ARMY OF
NORTHERN VIRGINIA

Edited and with an introduction
by Robert E. L. Krick

The University of Alabama Press
Tuscaloosa

Typeface: Bembo

∞

The paper on which this book is printed meets the minimum requirements of
American National Standard for Information Sciences-Permanence of Paper for
Printed Library Materials, ANSI Z39.48-1984.

Library of Congress Cataloging-in-Publication Data

Chamberlaine, William Wilson, 1836–1923.
Memoirs of the Civil War between the northern and southern sections of the
United States of America, 1861 to 1865 / William W. Chamberlaine.
p. cm. — (Seeing the elephant : southern eyewitnesses to the Civil War)
Originally published: Washington, D.C. : Press of Byron S. Adams, 1912.
Includes index.
ISBN 978-0-8173-5635-4 (pbk. : alk. paper) — ISBN 978-0-8173-8507-1
(electronic)
1. United States—History—Civil War, 1861–1865—Personal narratives,
Confederate. 2. Confederate States of America. Army. Virginia Infantry
Regiment, 6th. 3. United States—History—Civil War, 1861–1865—Regimental
histories. 4. Virginia—History—Civil War, 1861–1865—Regimental histories.
5. United States—History—Civil War, 1861–1865—Artillery operations. 6.
Virginia—History—Civil War, 1861–1865—Artillery operations. I. Title.
E605.C44 2011
973.7'82—dc22

2010051459

Cover: Desperate circumstances at Sharpsburg led to a memorable stand by
Confederate artillerists. Don Troiani's "Battery Longstreet" re-creates the scene
near W. W. Chamberlaine's personal heroics at the Piper Farm, marked by a small
stone monument that survives today next to the Hagerstown Pike.

Contents

Contents

Editor's Preface

"Seeing the Elephant: Southern Eyewitnesses to the Civil War" presents a range of firsthand testimony to modern readers. Primarily focused on reprinting accounts by Confederates or other Southerners who experienced the conflict, the series will occasionally offer works by foreign or Northern observers. Collectively, the volumes will carry readers across an expansive landscape of war, illuminating battles and campaigns as well as how the conflict shaped lives in cities and the countryside. Witnesses will include men and women, some prominent others less so, whose letters, diaries, and reminiscences convey immediate and retrospective attitudes and opinions. New introductions will enhance the value of each account, providing details about the authors and placing the books within the broader literature on the war. Indexes prepared for these editions will enable scholars and lay readers to make the most of the texts.

William Wilson Chamberlaine's *Memoirs of the Civil War,* though relatively little known because of its scarcity in the original edition, contains a great deal of valuable information and engaging narrative passages. A Virginian whose Confederate career included time in an infantry regiment early in the war, Chamberlaine saw his greatest service as a staff officer attached to Brigadier General Reuben Lindsay Walker, who commanded the Third Corps artillery in the Army of Northern Virginia. His book includes excellent material regarding, among other things, the duties carried out by staff officers, the operation of Confederate conscription, and the role of artillery in Robert E. Lee's campaigns. The text is especially lively and revealing about a number of famous battles—including the Seven Days, Antietam, where Chamberlaine distinguished himself and was wounded, and the Wilderness, where he had a memorable encounter with Lee. *Memoirs of the Civil War* benefits in this edition from a perceptive introduction by Robert E. L. Krick. Its intrinsic merits should earn widespread and well-deserved attention from readers interested in the storied operations of the Army of Northern Virginia.

Gary W. Gallagher
Charlottesville, Virginia
July 31, 2009

Editor's Introduction

William Wilson Chamberlaine, Virginia infantryman, artillerist, and staff officer, might be the only published memoirist from the Army of Northern Virginia who is better known today for a monument than for his book. A modest slab of stone near the mouth of the Piper Farm lane at Sharpsburg commemorates Chamberlaine's heroics there on September 17, 1862. Thousands of visitors see that marker annually, yet few know of his valuable reminiscences published exactly fifty years later. This first major reissue of *Memoirs of the Civil War* should redress that imbalance.

Chamberlaine's antebellum experiences are not very different from those of other Virginia soldier-authors. In fact, his own career path bore a noticeable resemblance to that of his Norfolk chum Walter H. Taylor, famous today for having been R. E. Lee's adjutant during the entire four years of the Civil War. Born in Norfolk on October 16, 1836, Chamberlaine represented a distinguished family with ancient ties to Virginia. His great-grandfather and grandfather (a shipbuilder) each fought the British in successive wars. William's father, Richard Henry Chamberlaine, had no opportunity for military service and confined himself to banking in his native Norfolk.[1]

As a boy William attended the Norfolk Military Academy in company with many other future Confederate officers. He moved on to Hampden-Sidney College for the 1852–53 school year. Chamberlaine left the college after just one year, though it is unlikely that family finances prompted his departure. Perhaps his family felt that William already had received a satisfactory education for someone not planning to read law or practice medicine. Whatever the reason, his academic career ended before his seventeenth birthday. He spent the next two years as a clerk in Norfolk before joining his father's bank—"R. H. Chamberlaine & Sons"—in 1855.[2]

Five years later the final census before the Civil War found William as a well-to-do bachelor in Norfolk, sharing a house with a U.S. Navy clerk but living next door to his brother George Chamberlaine. The census reported William's worth as $2,600 in real estate and $8,600 in personal estate. His circumstances—age, education, lineage, and occupation, in particular—made William W. Chamberlaine a perfect specimen of the sort of man who became a staff officer in the Army of Northern Virginia. Many of his peers in Norfolk fit the same profile, including the Taylor brothers, the Walke brothers, and Giles B. Cooke, several of whom are mentioned often in Chamberlaine's reminiscences. To some of them, at least, he was known as "Billy" Chamberlaine.[3]

In *Memoirs* Chamberlaine recounts the process by which he rose through the ranks, from a non-commissioned officer in a local prewar company to a member of the Sixth Virginia Infantry. Official documents show that he enlisted as a first lieutenant in what became Company G of that regiment on April 19, 1861, and that he became acting regimental adjutant by June 30. Five months later he commanded his company in the absence of its captain, and continued in that role until at least April 1862. During that period he attempted to secure a commission in the regular army of the Confederate States (as opposed to the provisional, or wartime army). A solid endorsement from Colonel Francis H. Smith praised Chamberlaine as "one of the best + most intelligent officers of this command," but the application never produced the desired commission.[4]

Chamberlaine says little in his reminiscences about the controversial reorganization that afflicted all Confederate units in April 1862. He merely notes that in May 1862 he was not in the army, "having in mind the intention of becoming the Adjutant of a new Regiment," or perhaps of joining a new artillery company being raised by Stapleton Crutchfield, an officer of his acquaintance. Lieutenant Chamberlaine had, in fact, declined reelection during the army reorganization in April and was dropped from the regiment effective May 1. There is no further evidence about this. Some officers refused to electioneer for positions they already held. Chamberlaine might have fallen into that category; or, he could have been too confident about his prospects elsewhere.

Either way, he returned to the Sixth Virginia after a short absence, having been elected to fill a vacant second lieutenancy on May 18.[5]

Lieutenant Chamberlaine witnessed the Seven Days battles, particularly Malvern Hill, where the brigade, in which his regiment served (General William Mahone's), saw fierce action. His account of that frantic week east of Richmond is useful. Although no large body of his wartime letters is known to exist, a letter Chamberlaine wrote in July 1862 to an acquaintance survives to supplement his later reminiscences. It nicely corroborates many of the statements he made in his book half a century later. But the private wartime letter is more frank. "The straggling from our army was shocking, distressing," he wrote. Chamberlaine also praised the valor of his Deep South comrades during the Seven Days, albeit in a back-handed manner. "Those Georgians and Mississippians look ragged & dirty, & the officers look stupid & careless, but just see them on the field of battle & I tell you, you will form the highest opinion. At least of their Courage & Patriotism."[6]

A fortunate assignment for special duty in Franklin County, Virginia, kept the lieutenant away from the army for the balance of the summer, and he missed the fighting at Second Manassas and Crampton's Gap. Chamberlaine's well-developed sense of duty prodded him to pursue the army into Maryland in September 1862, after the completion of his special detail in central Virginia. His tenacity allowed him, by his own account, to arrive just in time to participate in the battle at Sharpsburg. The carnage along Antietam Creek had few positive consequences, yet for Chamberlaine the battle provided an opportunity for personal distinction. His initiative in salvaging an abandoned cannon, patching together an improvised crew of Georgia infantrymen, and firing shells at short range into waves of advancing Federals near the Piper Farm, impressed bystanders. Chamberlaine describes the episode in valuable detail in chapter four of this volume. A slight scratch on his nose at Sharpsburg produced a noticeable scar, which turned out to be a small price to pay for a lifetime of accolades.[7]

His success with the artillery must have inspired Chamberlaine to make another effort at securing a commission in that branch of the service. On September 25 he wrote to the Secretary of War asking for that and supplying ringing endorsements from prominent army officers to buttress his case. Colonel William Parham, who commanded

Mahone's brigade at Sharpsburg, praised Chamberlaine as "an accomplished officer—steady, prompt & reliable." "With only two men to aid him he handled with such effect a piece of artillery . . . as to induce high acknowledgement of its service by Gen. Longstreet." Colonel William Gibson, in charge of an adjacent Georgia brigade, added a particularly effective testimonial. The colonel watched the whole episode, thought its value to the patchwork Confederate defense "was incalculable," and "without even having seen him before to know him, I feel no hesitancy in recommending him for promotion in the Artillery Service, or wherever else true courage, Bravery & coolness in action may entitle one." General Cadmus M. Wilcox also wrote on Chamberlaine's behalf. He admitted that he did not see the lieutenant's heroics, but had heard about them from others.

Despite the strong endorsements, Chamberlaine's application produced no immediate results. He continued to command his infantry company during the autumn of 1862. A fortunate opportunity at Fredericksburg in December finally provided the opening he sought, and on either December 14 or 15, William W. Chamberlaine reported for temporary duty to the artillery company commanded by Benjamin Huger Jr., which marked the start of a twenty-eight-month connection with the army's artillery.

After two months with Huger, Chamberlaine moved over to headquarters of the Second Corps artillery, where he served as the acting adjutant for his friend Crutchfield, the chief of that branch. Chamberlaine remained in that position for the balance of the war, serving under Crutchfield only for a few weeks and then directly at the side of Brigadier General Reuben Lindsay Walker until April 1865. His position as adjutant meant that he interacted with many of the army's leaders and stayed well informed about events. His only promotion came in October 1863, when his patron General Walker initiated paperwork to make Chamberlaine's appointment a permanent one. The army's bureaucratic artillery chief, William N. Pendleton, echoed Walker's kind words about Chamberlaine, writing that it would be "unjust not to grant him the rank due to the position he so well filled + so fully earned by gallantry." Effective October 23, 1863, Chamberlaine became a captain with the title of Assistant Adjutant General of the Third Corps artillery.[8]

In a period covering less than two years of the war, Chamberlaine met and married Matilda Hughes Dillard. Their courtship is described superficially in *Memoirs*. Early in the volume Chamberlaine reminds his readers that Confederates from Norfolk and elsewhere on Virginia's lower peninsula suffered permanent separation from their homes during the war years. The forlorn condition of Texas and Louisiana soldiers stranded in the Army of Northern Virginia seems obvious, but one rarely hears mention of the similar plight of southeastern Virginians. When the army abandoned Norfolk in May 1862 it was Chamberlaine's last glimpse of his home until sometime in 1865. Most of his family probably never even met his bride until after the war, by which time the couple already had an infant daughter.[9]

After Appomattox the ex-Confederate took his family to Norfolk and began rebuilding his life. He did not return to the banking business immediately. A city directory for 1866 shows Billy Chamberlaine as an "auctioneer and real estate broker" at 17 Roanoke Square, living at 12 South Cumberland Street. After six months in that profession, he returned to banking and soon thereafter established The Citizens Bank of Norfolk, where he served as cashier into the 1870s. The 1870 census reveals that Chamberlaine already was remarkably well off under the circumstances. The census listed his personal estate at $12,000 and his real estate at $16,000. His brother George continued to live next door, just as he had before the war.[10]

As time passed the old Confederate's influence grew in Norfolk. He was president of yet another bank in his hometown, and had an affiliation (usually as comptroller) with at least a half-dozen different area railroads. Chamberlaine superintended the construction of the city's first light and power plant, and subsequently served as president of the Norfolk Electric Light Company. He occupied responsible positions with the local water department, and even filled a seat on the Norfolk City Council for one term.

Predictably enough in a man so active, Chamberlaine showed a consistent, long-term interest in Confederate veterans' affairs, in battlefields, and in history. A posthumous biographical sketch reported that "Until his death he was a student of military science and of the events of the Civil War." When John Bigelow's mammoth *Chancellorsville* reached press in 1910, its author thanked Chamberlaine for assistance in the preparation of the book. Chamberlaine also served as a vice-president of The Chamberlain Association of America, and was the only one of the sixteen men in that position in 1908 who had the vowel at the end of the surname. Notable Civil War general Joshua L. Chamberlain was the group's president at that time.[11]

When he retired in 1909, Chamberlaine moved with his wife from Norfolk to Washington, D.C., where they spent the remainder of their lives. He continued to play the role of an old Confederate with zeal, taking "great interest in the organization and membership" of the local United Confederate Veterans camp, while retaining his "unceasing interest and connection with the Grand Camp of Virginia Veterans." In 1921 his peers elevated him to the rank of brigadier general in their organization, and made him the commander of the various dwindling camps in the region.[12]

It was during that period, in 1917, that Chamberlaine's friends received permission to erect a granite marker on the Sharpsburg battlefield to commemorate his actions there fifty-five years earlier. "Owing to the rigid rules laid down by the United States government," grumbled one veteran, the marker "tells the story of this incident as a wood sawyer might boast of a specially pecuniary job of half a cord of firewood sawed and split in record time." The terse inscription does not even name Chamberlaine, referring to him only as "a second lieutenant of the 6th Virginia Infantry." But his heroics and the story of the marker received considerable attention in the national veterans magazine, and in more recent guidebooks to the battlefield.[13]

Chamberlaine died at his home in Washington on October 19, 1923, three days after his eighty-seventh birthday, and with his son at his bedside. The few remaining members of the local United Confederate Veterans camp, with whom he had forged such a close connection, issued the customary sorrowful resolutions. The funeral occurred at his house, followed by interment at Glenwood Cemetery.[14]

There is little definitive evidence about the motivation behind Chamberlaine's preparation of his memoirs. In his introduction, he lamented the absence of written material from the pens of his fighting forebears, and vowed to do better for his heirs. By the time the book reached press in 1912, Chamberlaine had been retired from his hectic civilian life for three years. Perhaps preparing his reminiscences helped fill the sudden void in his time. His association with the United Confederate Veterans organization in Washington, D.C., may also have inspired him to record his memories for posterity. Yet another contributing factor could have been some writing he did in 1909, at someone else's request. In January of that year he prepared a short account of the retreat to Appomattox and sent it to an interested party in Richmond. That episode may have stimulated in him a taste for the work of converting cherished memories into chronological prose for the world to see and enjoy.[15]

The press of Byron S. Adams issued Memoirs of the Civil War in 1912. Chamberlaine probably selected Adams because of its proximity to his new residence, and perhaps because of its experience with at least two other similar books with Civil War content. The print run must have been small, as copies today infrequently appear on the market. In the rare instances when a solid copy appears, it usually commands several thousand dollars. Adams issued the 138-page book in a dark red cloth with a plain manila dust jacket.[16]

Further proof of the limited circulation afforded Chamberlaine's Memoirs comes from its lack of public notice in 1912. The trade journals did not review it, nor did the Washington Post. Confederate Veteran magazine usually could be relied upon to provide warm endorsements of veterans' books, yet it also was silent. The absence of publicity strengthens the suspicion that Chamberlaine really did get the book into print for family and friends, rather than as an exercise in scholarship.

The book's scarcity has prevented it from garnering much attention in modern times too. Not unexpectedly, the pioneer Confederate historian Douglas Southall Freeman knew of it and admired it, naming it as one of a handful of books essential for a student "to understand the morale of an army. . . . From those narratives one often gets color and incident and a thousand touches that lighten the unrelieved seriousness of official reports." An ill-informed 1960s assessment of Chamberlaine's Memoirs in a popular bibliography characterized the book as "of no tangible value" due to "The author's reliance on an unreliable memory, plus his many factual inaccuracies."[17]

Memoirs actually is remarkable for its even tone and precision. There are mistakes and a few gaps in the narrative, but the errors are broad ones, appearing infrequently. A very close reading of the entire volume produces the suspicion that Chamberlaine had a journal or some other data to consult during the preparation of his book. His tale is a straightforward military autobiography, with only a few diversions into analysis. There is little if any reflection or introspection. It is a collection of stories and memories, enlivened by his connection with some of the war's most famous soldiers.

There are several sections of Chamberlaine's book that are unique, or at least unusual. His frank discussion of a friendly fire episode east of Richmond in June 1862 offers rare insight into an underreported reality of Civil War tactics. His frightening encounter with a poisonous snake—probably a copperhead—also is a singular anecdote. One rarely sees accounts from snake-bitten Civil War soldiers. Readers looking for material on weightier subjects will enjoy Chamberlaine's anecdotal evidence about the failure of the Confederate substitution system. His personal experiences in chasing draft dodgers in central Virginia are useful, as are his encounters with army commander R. E. Lee, especially at the Battle of the Wilderness.

The overarching value of *Memoirs of the Civil War* comes from its author's connection with the Third Corps artillery. The published letters of J. Hampden Chamberlayne and the memoir of William T. Poague are classics from that particular section of the army, but literate source material from that corps lags far behind what is available from either of the army's other two corps. Perhaps because of that, Chamberlaine's patron, General R. Lindsay Walker, is not a well-known figure. This Chamberlaine memoir also illuminates the diverse activities of a staff officer, both in camp and on the battlefield. His criticism of Confederate staff work during the Seven Days battles, while not a unique point of view, carries extra credence because of his own extensive experience in that field.

Chamberlaine wrote these memoirs, he said, with the modest goal of informing his children and their descendants about his role in the great national conflict. He accomplished that in an entertaining style, mixing occasional drollery and soldier humor with a chronological retelling of his experiences. Captain Chamberlaine missed only three major battles between May 1862 and April 1865. From the book's highlight at Sharpsburg to its denouement at Appomattox, he succeeded in recounting enough significant eyewitness detail to make his *Memoirs* worthy of wide distribution.

Robert E. L. Krick
Glen Allen, Virginia

NOTES

1. William's parents were Richard Henry and Mary Eliza Wilson Chamberlaine. Their 1831 marriage led to seven children. William's mother died in 1847, and his father remarried in 1851, eventually producing four half-siblings for William. Several of the Chamberlaine boys saw Confederate service, including George Chamberlaine of the 9th Virginia Infantry. Lists of the various brothers and sisters appear in several biographical sketches of William, most notably *Eminent and Representative Men of Virginia and the District of Columbia of the Nineteenth Century* (Madison, Wis.: Brant & Fuller, 1893), 420–22; and *The National Cyclopaedia of American Biography* (New York: James T. White & Company, 1958), 42:372–73. A photograph and biographical sketch of George Chamberlaine, William's older brother, is in *Confederate Veteran* 20 (1912):125. Like Chamberlaine, Walter Taylor attended the Norfolk Military Academy, spent a very short time in college (in Taylor's case the Virginia Military Institute), and then worked as a bank clerk in prewar Norfolk. See Robert E. L. Krick, *Staff Officers in Gray* (Chapel Hill: Univ. of North Carolina Press, 2003), 283. Thanks to Jack Bales at the Mary Washington College Library in Fredericksburg, Virginia, for pointing out the Chamberlaine material in the *National Cyclopaedia*.

2. *National Cyclopaedia of American Biography*, 42:372; *Eminent and Representative Men*, 420–21. In Chamberlaine's day his college was spelled Hampden-Sidney. Today it is Hampden-Sydney.

3. Norfolk County census, 1860, p. 357, National Archives, Washington, D.C.; Giles B. Cooke diary, July 28, 1864, Virginia Historical Society, Richmond, Virginia.

4. Chamberlaine's military service records are in "Compiled Service Records of Confederate Soldiers Who Served in Organizations from the State of Virginia," M324, Roll 436, National Archives, and "Compiled Service Records of Confederate General and Staff Officers," M331, Roll 52, National Archives.

5. Sixth Virginia Compiled Service Record, M324, Roll 436, National Archives.

6. Letter of "W. W. C." to "My dear Mac," July 24, 1862, in Alexander M. McPheeters Collection, Perkins Library, Duke University, Durham, North Carolina.

7. *Confederate Veteran* 26 (1918): 239-40.

8. Compiled Service Record in M331, Roll 52, National Archives; Sixth Virginia Compiled Service Record, M324, Roll 436, National Archives. In order to keep the paperwork straight, Chamberlaine had to be discharged from the Sixth Virginia Infantry. The precise date is lost, but that occurred about December 1863. Although Chamberlaine began his artillery duty with the Second Corps, the portion that he served with became part of the Third Corps in the summer of 1863 during the army's realignment. His job and circumstances did not change.

9. The marriage occurred on April 20, 1864, at Trinity Episcopal Church in Rocky Mount, Virginia. The couple had three children: Mary Wilson Chamberlaine, Anne Dillard Chamberlaine, and William Chamberlaine. The son attended the U. S. Military Academy and became a brigadier general; the daughters married and gave Billy Chamberlaine grandchildren, including a grandson who also served in the U. S. Army. Marriage and baptism records are on-line at http://www.trinityepiscopalrmva.com/ in 2008. See also Norfolk *Virginian-Pilot and the Norfolk Landmark,* October 20, 1923, and *Eminent and Representative Men,* 421. *National Cyclopaedia of American Biography,* 373, differs on the marriage date, giving April 21 instead of April 20. In his July 1862 letter (McPheeters Papers, Duke), Chamberlaine writes about the difficulties and uncertainties of communicating with his family in Norfolk.

10. *Norfolk City and Business Directory for 1866* (Baltimore: Webb and Fitzgerald, 1866); *The National Cyclopaedia of American Biography,* 372; 1870 Norfolk County census, p. 86, National Archives.

11. *National Cyclopaedia of American Biography,* 373; John Bigelow, Jr., *The Campaign of Chancellorsville* (New Haven: Yale University Press, 1910), xv; *The Chamberlain Association of America* (New York: The Grafton Press, 1908), 82.

12. *Washington Post,* October 20, 1923; *Norfolk Ledger-Dispatch,* October 20, 1923; *Confederate Veteran* 32 (1924): 29.

13. "Gunners of the 6th Va. Infy.," in *Blue & Gray Magazine* (October 1995): 55–57; *Confederate Veteran* 26 (1918): 73–74, 239-40. Page 239 of the latter citation includes a late-life photograph of a soldierly looking Chamberlaine, standing beside a fellow veteran from Mahone's Virginia brigade.

14. Chamberlaine lived at 1806 Wyoming Avenue, NW, at the time of his death. *Washington Post,* October 20, 1923; *Norfolk Ledger-Dispatch,* October 20, 1923; Norfolk *Virginian-Pilot and the Norfolk Landmark,* Oct. 20, 1923. The latter newspaper reproduced an old-age photograph of Chamberlaine, apparently

attired in his United Confederate Veterans uniform. The resolutions from his comrades were published in *Confederate Veteran* 32 (1924): 29. They include this startling exaggeration, typical of such things: "Probably no soldier or officer rendered more efficient service than did this veteran."

15. The Museum of the Confederacy in Richmond has a typescript of Chamberlaine's 1909 account that bears the title "Personal Recollections of the Retreat of the Reserve Artillery of the Army of Northern Virginia, from Amelia C. H. Va., April 5th, to April 9th, 1865." Although that version shares some factual and anecdotal points with the published *Memoirs*, it is considerably different.

16. Other similar titles from Adams are Joseph Packard's *Recollections of a Long Life* (1902) and Marcus Benjamin's *Washington During War Time* (1902). Adams also produced the memoirs of Anson Mills, a prominent Indian fighter, in 1918. The press still operates in Washington. An April 2008 enquiry with Adams, asking about its history and the potential for any business files on Chamberlaine's book was not successful.

17. Freeman's remarks are in his foreword to *John Dooley: Confederate Soldier*, ed. Joseph T. Durkin (Washington, D. C.: Georgetown University Press, 1945), x. The inexplicably obtuse review appears in Allan Nevins et al., *Civil War Books, A Critical Bibliography*, 2 vols. (Baton Rouge: Lousiana State University Press, 1967), 1:68. Freeman placed Chamberlaine's book among classics by John Casler, David Johnston, Ned Moore, and John Worsham. But he damaged his own analysis somewhat by stressing that the books he recommended were by "privates or sergeants of Lee's Army," when in fact Chamberlaine was a captain, and had little in common with the Caslers and Moores of the army.

Introduction

The intention of these memoirs is to furnish my children and their descendants, in printed form, an account of the experience of the writer during the War waged from 1861 to 1865 by the Northern States of the Union against the Government set up by the Southern States, in order to force the latter to return to the Union. During its existence, the group of Southern States took the name of the Confederate States of America. My Great Grandfather was a Lieutenant serving with the Barrens in the Navy of the Colony of Virginia during the Revolutionary War of 1776 and his son, my paternal Grandfather, served with the Militia in the war with England in 1812, both were named George Chamberlaine. Having often wished they had left an account of their experiences in the Service, I determined that if my descendants had a desire to know something of my Experience in the War of 1861 to 1865, they would have it in permanent form. I have now reached a ripe old age, but my memory of the events related is clear, and I have a few contemporaries left, who served in the same Army and perhaps some of them may take an interest in reading this account of scenes familiar to themselves. If they find the personal pronoun used very often, they should remember that this is a statement of my personal recollections and excuse its frequent use.

THE AUTHOR

Chapter I

Service with the Infantry

In the year 1859 (I was then twenty-three years old) John Brown attempted to array the negroes in Northern Virginia against the white people, and with his followers, mostly negroes, took possession of Harper's Ferry. Troops were dispatched to the scene by the U. S. Government, as there was an Arsenal at Harpers Ferry, and after a short struggle John Brown and his followers were taken prisoners and turned over to the authorities of Virginia. There were some casualties during the fight, which was conducted by Col. R. E. Lee assisted by Lieut. J. E. B. Stuart, both of the Regular U. S. Cavalry and an officer of the U. S. Marines, on the part of the Government. That attempt of John Brown excited the Military spirit of the young men and Volunteer Companies were formed in different places in Virginia.

At Norfolk, Va., a Company was formed by the young gentlemen of the City, and was called the Southern Guard and Company F. I had attended the Norfolk Military Academy in my youth, and was quite proficient in the School of the Company and of the Battalion. An election was held for officers, both Commissioned and Non-Commissioned, and I was elected Corporal. The Company was commanded by Captain Edmond Bradford, formerly an officer of the U. S. Artillery, with Harry Williamson, who had served in the War with Mexico, as First Lieutenant, and R. C. Taylor, a graduate of the Virginia Military Institute, as Second Lieutenant. Walter H. Taylor was First Sergeant.

The Company was drilled and paraded during two years following. In the meantime Sergeant Taylor had been promoted, by election, to Second Lieutenant to fill a vacancy and I was made First Sergeant.

Then came the election of A. Lincoln as President. The Gulf States began to pass ordinances of Secession from the Union. In March following Lincoln was inaugurated and took his place at the head of the Government. Step by step in the next month acts were committed by the Seceded States and the U. S. Government which led to the War. A convention was in session at Richmond, Va. A majority of the members were opposed to Secession and great efforts were made to preserve peace, but when the President called upon the States for their quota of a force of seventy-five thousand men to coerce the Seceded States, the Virginia Convention decided to join the Gulf States and passed an ordinance of Secession. I was then staying at my father's house on E. Main Street, and that same night at twelve o'clock, there was a ring of the front door bell. It was a messenger with an order for me to assemble Company F at the Armory. Before 2:00 A. M., the Company having assembled, it was marched by Lieut. Williamson by way of Ghent to Fort Norfolk. The distance was two miles. At Ghent the command was given to halt and load. The muskets being loaded we proceeded to Fort Norfolk.

On the way rumors were heard that other Volunteer Companies had preceded us to the Fort and had been attacked by U. S. Marines from the Navy Yard and cut to pieces. On arrival it was found that the rumors were false. Several Companies had reached the Fort and were removing ammunition; that being a Magazine of the U. S. Navy. During the rest of that night and all the next day, the work of removing the ammunition went on. There were some alarms during the day, but no effort was made by the U. S. officers to stop the work. There were several U. S. Ships at the Navy Yard, one mile distant, and one shell dropped near the Fort, I believe, would have caused a cessation of the work, because it might have blown up the whole Fort, by setting fire to the ammunition. By sunset the large stock of powder and shell had been hauled back one mile and piled on the land of Mr. Robert Searles.

The men of our Company had now been at work about twenty hours and were much fatigued, so they were marched back to the Armory; when they arrived there the U. S. Navy Yard had been abandoned by the Ships, including the "Pawnee," which arrived during the afternoon, and was in flames. The Company remained on duty at the Armory until early in the month of May. Meantime Lieut. Williamson was promoted to be Captain, and I to be Lieutenant, by election.

It was ordered to Craney Island. Lieut. W. H. Taylor was called to the Staff of General R. E. Lee, and E. M. Hardy and Duncan Robertson elected Lieutenants.

The garrison of Craney Island was reinforced from time to time until the force reached the total of nine hundred men. Earth works were raised along the front of the Island and cannon from the Navy Yard mounted. Company "F" held the right of the line, at the point where stood an old block house built of brick and the earth works enclosed the space. Captain Charles Dimmock, of the Engineer Corps, was in charge of the construction of the earth works and Captain H. Williamson was detailed to assist him. Our first commanding officer was Col. Richardson, an appointee of Governor Letcher. Captain Wm. McBlair and Lieut. Commander Fitzgerald of the Navy were also on duty there. I was detailed as Adjutant of the Post. Afterwards Col. Richardson was ordered to other duty and Col. F. H. Smith, of the Virginia Military Institute, was placed in command. He was accompanied by Lieut. Col. Preston and Major S. Crutchfield. At my request I was relieved from the position of Adjutant and returned to duty with Company "F," which I commanded (the Captain having been detailed as stated), until the month of May in the year 1862. Dr. H. M. Nash was the Surgeon of the Command. The Command was drilled regularly as Infantry and also at the Naval Guns. The young ladies of Norfolk sent a deputation to the Island and presented Company "F" with a very handsome silk Confederate States Flag, which was received with a most agreeable but solemn ceremony. The Enemy occupied Fort Monroe and Newport News, and had several Men-of-War at each place. Meantime the force at Norfolk and vicinity was organized into Regiments and Brigades. General Benjamin Huger commanded the Department and Generals Blanchard and Mahone the Brigades. In that organization our Company became Company "G" of the 6th Virginia Infantry. Many times a small steamer came from Old Point displaying a flag of truce and our Commanding Officer would send a barge with an officer to meet the same. The Steamboat William Selden, Captain T. S. Southgate, made two regular trips from Norfolk to the Island. Sometimes she was replaced by the Kahukee, Captain Babel Taylor. One morning in the fall Lieut. Duncan Robertson and I went to the wharf on the arrival of the William Selden. As the lines were cast off for her departure, a newsboy named Bremmer made a leap to reach the deck of the boat, but missed and fell into the water at the end of the pier. The water was deep and he sank. A heaving line was thrown to him as he rose, but he failed to get it; then several pieces of cord wood. He sank out of sight twice. I could not bear seeing the youth drown, so I removed my uniform coat and plunged into the water with the purpose of taking the loose end of the heavy line and passing it to him. A man on the deck of the steamer held one end of the line, but the steamer drifted away. I swam to the loose end, then turned and swam to the boy who was struggling to keep above the surface of the water with a stick of wood, which was not enough to sustain him. I placed the line in his hands and it sustained him, then I swam to the side of the steamer and seized the loop of one of her large lines hanging from her sides. Thus young Bremmer and myself were supported by lines and we remained in that position until a small boat was rowed from the shore and took us both to the Island. The water was very cold, so I proceeded at once to my quarters and remained in bed for several hours and there were no bad results from my plunge. Bremmer's father was a member of the Company commanded by Captain Wilbern and was a tailor by trade. He was grateful for what I had done for his young son and took my clothes and dried and pressed them nicely. In the afternoon a flag of truce boat was sighted and I received an order to go out in the barge to meet it. I promptly obeyed the order and had the pleasure of escorting three ladies to Norfolk who had been permitted to pass through the lines. They were Mrs. General Wm. Martin, Mrs. C. M. Fry, formerly Miss Leigh, daughter of Benj. Watkins Leigh, of Virginia, and Mrs. Harvey, wife of an officer of the English Army, who was in the Federal Service and was among the missing at the Battle of Balls' Bluff near Leesburg, Va. Mrs. Harvey was permitted to pass through the lines in search of her husband. I have never heard whether she found him.

By that flag of truce, also came the news of the seizure of Mason and Slidell on their way to Europe to represent the Confederate States. They had taken passage at Havana on an English Passenger Ship which was intercepted by a United States Man-of-War and Messrs. Mason and Slidell taken as prisoners.

Towards the end of the year Colonel Smith was relieved and went back to the Virginia Military Institute, accompanied by Lieut. Col. Preston; Major Crutchfield was transferred to a regiment serving in the Western part of Virginia. Lieut. Col. J. A. DéLagnel, the hero of the battle of Rich Mountain, just released from Fort LaFayette, New York Harbor, assumed command and Major Mark Hardin, from the Stonewall Brigade, took the place of Major S. Crutchfield. Col. DéLagnel had served in the 2nd Artillery of the U. S. Army and was a very accomplished officer and was highly esteemed by the garrison. That garrison was fortunate to have had so many excellent superior officers.

I turn aside for a moment from my own recollections to relate a story told me by Col. DéLagnel. When hostilities commenced he was on duty at the U. S. Arsenal at Fayetteville, N. C. The Arsenal was surrounded by a large force of North Carolina Soldiers and its surrender demanded. As it was manifestly useless to try to defend the place garrisoned by one Company, the Commanding Officer agreed to surrender, provided he would be permitted to march his Company away with their arms and baggage. Colors flying and drums beating, the Company was marched to the Steamboat landing and proceeded *to* the mouth of the Cape Fear River, and embarked on a schooner for New York City. They reached that place in due time, and then took a train for Washington, D. C. There the Company was turned over to the U. S. Authorities and DéLagnel handed in his resignation. His duty performed, he went to the Paymaster to settle his account, which was done, but to pay the balance due him up to that date, the Paymaster said he was ordered to give a draft on the funds which the U. S. Government had in the hands of the Officer of the Treasury at Charleston, S.C. The State of South Carolina having seceded, whatever funds had been there when hostilities commenced, were then held by the Confederate States Government. As he knew the draft would not be honored, DéLagnel refused to accept it. The balance remained to his credit until about 1886, when after the lapse of so many years it was finally recovered.

When Major Crutchfield left the Island Col. Smith directed an escort of two Companies to go to Norfolk with him. Captain R. C. Taylor's Company and our own formed the escort. That was the last time these Companies, as organizations, visited their native city.

In our Company, now Company "G" 6th Virginia Infantry, there were many of the dear friends of my youth. As it was composed of young men of intelligence, many of the best families of Norfolk, besides many who came from other parts of the State, a great many were eagerly sought for to fill responsible positions in the Confederate Army. My friend, John H. Sharp, was appointed Captain and Commissary of Subsistence. He accepted at first, but afterwards decided not to hold the position, and at his request my older brother, George Chamberlaine, was appointed in his place and was ordered to the Post of Craney Island. My friend, Theoderick A. Williams, was appointed Sergeant Major of the regiment, and as the Colonel, Wm. Mahone, and most of the companies were stationed at an entrenched camp near Norfolk, he reported at that Camp. There were four brothers of the Urquhart family from Southampton Co., F. M. Whitehurst, from Princess Anne Co., two brothers, Robinson, from Washington, D. C., also two brothers of the Todd family, Henry and George M., I. Barry King and others. On the 8th of March, 1862, the "Iron Clad Virginia," rebuilt from the U. S. Ship "Merrimac," came down from the Navy Yard and passed our Fort on the way to Newport News. Colonel DéLagnel ordered the Command to Arms. The guns were manned and the result of the attack on the ships at Newport News was awaited with anxiety and excitement. Newport News, seven miles distant, is in plain sight of Craney Island, and the weather was perfectly clear. From our positions at our guns we could see all the maneuvers; could see the smoke of the guns, the sinking of the "Cumberland," the arrival of two Confederate Steamships from Richmond, and the attack on the "Congress." The "Virginia" was accompanied by the small armed ship "Beaufort" and several armed tug boats, all of which participated in the engagement. We saw the "Congress" hoist sails and attempt to slip away, but she ran aground near Newport News. After awhile we could see that she was on fire and was still burning, when fatigued by the excitement of the day, we fell asleep. We could see several of the U. S. Ships start towards Newport News to the aid of the "Congress." All, after having proceeded a short distance, returned to Old Point, except the "Minnesota," which ship ran aground about three miles and a half from Newport News, that is, about half way from Old Point. At dusk the Confederate ships anchored off Sewall's Point. Next morning, the 9th, we were up early and I was told the Magazine of the "Congress" exploded about 4:00 A. M., but it did not wake me. Soon after daylight the "Virginia" proceeded to attack the "Minnesota," still aground. I saw a shell strike a tug boat lying alongside of the "Minnesota," and an escape of steam. Then the "Monitor" appeared and an engagement followed between the "Virginia" and the "Monitor" which lasted several hours. We could see the shots rebound from the ironsides of both vessels. The engagement ceased, but we could not see well enough to determine the reason, as both vessels were constantly changing positions. It was said the "Monitor" moved into shoal water, where the "Virginia" with her deep draft of water could not follow. That afternoon the Confederate Ships went up to the Navy Yard. Some weeks after the "Virginia" accompanied by several small armed steamers, passed down towards Old Point and captured a transport.

The U. S. Vessels did not show any disposition to engage the Confederate Ships and the latter returned to the Navy Yard. In the spring of 1862, the Army of the Potomac was transferred from its line of defenses near Alexandria to a point on the Virginia Peninsula near York Town and commenced the siege of that place. On our side the regiments were reorganized. Elections were held according to the law in the Companies for Captain and Lieutenants, and then the Company officers were convened to elect Field Officers. H. Williamson was reelected Captain and E. M. Hardy, Duncan Robertson, and John T. Lester, Lieutenants of Company "G." When the Company Officers of the regiment were convened for the election of Field Officers, Major George T. Rogers was elected Colonel, Captain H. Williamson Lieut. Colonel, and Captain Robert B. Taylor, Major, of the 6th Virginia Regiment of Infantry.

Early in May, 1862, the Confederate troops were withdrawn from Norfolk and its vicinity and proceeded to Petersburg, Va. Early one morning my colored servant called at my father's house to inform me that the Federal forces were advancing on the City and the Confederate troops were leaving. I was not in the service at that time, having in mind the intention of becoming the Adjutant of a new Regiment, and in case that was not attained, to attach, myself to a Battery of Light Artillery to be raised by Major S. Crutchfield, who wished me to take the place of First Sergeant. Neither of those plans was carried out. A new Act of Congress forestalled the organization of the new Regiment and Major Crutchfield was appointed to a position on the Staff of Major General (Stonewall) Jackson. I went to Petersburg and lived at the Bolingbrooke Hotel two weeks, when I received a message from Captain Hardy that there was a vacant Lieutenancy in Company "G" and the Company desired me to fill it. I consented to the proposition and was duly elected and reported for duty to Col. Rogers at Drewry's Bluff, where Mahone's Brigade was in Camp. There the Brigade was on outpost duty below Fort Darling, which position was menaced by the Federal Gunboats. Towards the end of May the 6th Regiment was sent across the James River and attached to General Wise's Command, which was guarding the right flank of the Army under Gen. Jos. E. Johnson. On the 30th of May we saw President Davis and Gen. Jos. E, Johnson near our Camp examining the position. That night a very severe thunder storm came up with wind and a deluge of rain. Many tents were blown down and the camp flooded. The lightning was very sharp and the clouds hung over us for several hours. The Battle of Seven Pines occurred the next day. Seven Pines is about seven miles from Chapin's Bluff, where the 6th Virginia Regiment was at that time. The noise of that battle did not reach us. The other part of the Brigade was marched with Huger's Division to Seven Pines and was engaged on the second day of the battle—June 1st.

Chapter 2

Battles near Richmond

A few days afterwards some Federal Gunboats were seen coming up the river. General Wise's Command was deployed and marched in line of battle down the river towards them. The country is clear of trees, so each side could see the other. The Gunboats, however, did not fire a shot and soon withdrew and our command returned to Camp. A few days after the Regiment was ordered to rejoin the Brigade and marched to the outskirts of Richmond; then, by the Charles City Road, to the line of the Army commanded by General R. E. Lee, who succeeded General Jos. E. Johnson, who had been seriously wounded at the battle on the 31st of May. We were then in front of the Army of the Potomac under the Federal General Geo. B. McClellan. During our stay of several weeks at that position, the Regiment was frequently marched to the front, when the Brigade skirmished with the Enemy's outposts. Company "G" performed its tour of picket duty. On the 18th of June, in the afternoon, a report came to the Brigadier-General that a Federal Regiment was on the Charles City Road, marching towards our line. He ordered the 41st Virginia to take an old road running parallel nearly to the main road, and the first battalion of the 6th Virginia to proceed by a similar road on the south of the main road. The plan was to surround the Federal Regiment and capture or defeat it. Company "G" was in the first battalion. The troops started and felt their way slowly towards the enemy's front. They had to pass through the advanced line of pickets. The leading Company of our Battalion had originally the name of Manchester Grays and wore jackets and light blue trousers. One of the advanced pickets saw one of the Grays and taking him for a Federal soldier, fired at and wounded him severely. That caused some delay and finally, after advancing two miles, a shot was fired; from where, no one knew at the time, which wounded two men of our Company, Privates Wise and Fletcher. We were ordered to lie down. Fletcher was alongside of me. I bound up his wound with my pocket handkerchief—he was struck on the knee. After lying down a few moments, no other shot being fired, we were ordered to form line. As we got up, I saw following our Battalion, the 2nd Battalion, led by Major R. B. Taylor, quite near us and just beyond a slight elbow in the road. The main Charles City Road was supposed to be a very short distance to our left, and the Federal Regiment on that road. As soon as we rose to our feet a tremendous discharge of musketry was poured into us. We laid down quickly, and the firing was kept up for several minutes. I heard Major Taylor give the order "Fix Bayonets." I supposed the discharge came from the Federal Regiment. Some twenty-eight men were killed or wounded. Very soon afterwards we were marched slowly back to the Camp. The picket line was passed in safety—much to my surprise—for night had fallen at the time of the firing. The next day a detail was sent to the place, the dead were buried and the wounded cared for, but to this day I have never heard what became of Private Fletcher. Wise was brought back, but he was slightly lamed for life. Sergeant Major James W. Bell was with the 2nd Battalion and lost a part of his hand. The prevailing opinion was that there was no enemy there and the two Battalions had fired into each other, and I now incline to that opinion, but for a long time I believed we had been ambushed. Whether any Federal troops were there or not, there was another enemy present, just as much to be feared; that was the lack of experience of our Commanding Officer. He was then serving his apprenticeship, After a year or two of practice he became a good General Officer, indeed, one of the best Division Generals in the Army of Northern Virginia.

There was a law in force at that time, which allowed a soldier to be discharged upon providing a substitute. A member of our Company furnished a substitute and was discharged at that Camp. He left at once, but before he had reached the City of Richmond, eight miles distant, the substitute had deserted and I never heard anything more of him.

On the 25th of June an alarm was sounded, the Regiment at once paraded under arms. The enemy attacked our troops on the Williamsonburg Road about one mile to our left. The Brigade, with the exception of one Battalion of the 6th Virginia, proceeded to attack the left of the Federal force near King's School House and performed good service. Our Battalion, under Lieut. Col. Williamson, was marched on the road leading to the Williamsburg Road and held in reserve. Towards sunset an order came for us to join in the battle and we proceeded left in front. We passed a North Carolina Regiment, which had fled from the enemy and officers were trying to rally them. It was their first trial under fire. I have understood that after a little experience, it became an excellent Regiment. As we went towards the field, we met stragglers who said our force was cut to pieces, defeated, and so on. We kept on and advanced rear rank in front toward the enemy, who was in fact retreating. We reached the advanced line of troops and fired a volley after them. Darkness was coming on, and the battle was soon ended. The intention of the enemy was said afterwards to advance their picket line. It took several Brigades to make the attempt and as they were opposed by three Brigades of Confederates the result was a bloody battle.

General Lee had determined to attack McClellan's Army on the north side of the Chickahominy River on the next day, the 26th, and a large portion of the Army marched on that day to Mechanicsville, about ten miles from our position, leaving McGruders' and Huger's Divisions to hold the entrenchments which extended from the Charles City Road, through or near Seven Pines to the Chickahominy River. Opposed to those two Divisions was the bulk of the Federal Army. The force to which the 6th Virginia was attached was then on watch to protect the City of Richmond, while the rest of Lee's Army crossed the Chickahominy River to fight the battles of Ellyson's Mill and Cold Harbor. It was generally supposed that our two Divisions occupied a very critical position. At night we could hear the music of their bands and much shouting. On the afternoon of the 26th a battle was fought at Ellyson's Mill and on the 27th the first battle of Cold Harbor. Our Command was some ten miles from the latter place, with the Chickahominy River between. We passed the nights of the 26th, 27th, and 28th of June in some anxiety, expecting to be called to arms at any moment. But these three days and nights passed without any demonstration by the enemy in front of us. The next day, the 28th, was very hot, and about midday the Brigade was ordered to march by the Charles City Road to intercept the Federal Army marching towards the James River. About 7:00 P. M. the advance guard discovered Federal Troops at one of the crossings of White Oak Swamp. A slight skirmish took place, and the Federals retired to seek another crossing. The Brigade proceeded down the road a little farther when, night having fallen, it bivouacked in the woods on the side of the road. Soon after a Federal Cavalry patrol trotted up towards our position. The men opened fire on the patrol and almost destroyed it; a few turned and escaped. That was a valuable lesson to us, who were then without experience. That patrol should have been surrounded and captured. In the first place there was no use shooting their men. In the second, valuable information of the enemy's movements might have been obtained. There was no further excitement that night. The next morning the Adjutant of the 6th Virginia was reported sick and I was sent for to take his place, and the 6th Virginia was the advance guard. The Colonel was also taken sick and Lieut. Col. Williamson commanded the Regiment. After proceeding a mile or two we came to a swamp which the road crossed; in crossing the little bridge a shot was fired by a vidette of the enemy. We pushed across and found the road obstructed by huge trees, which had been cut down and fallen across. Farther on other pine trees were found across the road, then more. The Regiment was deployed on the right of the road and advanced, bayonets charged. On the left of the road the 49th Virginia, Col. Wm. Smith, advanced in the same way. After passing four obstructions Col. Williamson sent me to inform General Mahone of the progress made. I found him sitting on a tree at the first obstruction. He said, very well, tell the Colonel to go on. About that time Captain Carter Williams went forward to reconnoiter and, bringing back a drum, said he had not seen any enemy in front. We had been passing through woods, but now on the left of us was an open field called Brackett's Field; the right of the road was wooded. A portion of Moorman's Battery was brought up, going around the obstruction, and went into battery in the field near the road and opened fire. Captain Williams had not seen the enemy, but they were very near, lying down in line of battle, with two batteries ready for action, which replied to Moorman's guns immediately. From what I have read since I believe they were Upton's and Hexamer's batteries, and they had a part of another, making fourteen guns. Moorman's two guns were soon withdrawn, badly damaged, and the firing from those batteries was continued for an hour or more. Another Regiment was brought up and the Confederate Infantry laid there under that terrific fire without making any movement, losing many men. When the firing slackened a slight change was made in the position of the 6th Virginia, it was drawn back a little; then darkness came and firing ceased. Being young I did not know anything about the plans of the Generals, but supposed that our Command alone was confronted by the whole Federal Army. The facts were, as I have since learned, that General Thos. J. Jackson's troops were at the crossing of White Oak Swamp, not much more than one mile to our left, and General Longstreet, with his own and General A. P. Hill's division, were two or three miles to our right. The question arises, is it good policy to keep the Field and Company Officers in perfect ignorance of the plans and of the whereabouts of the other parts of the Army. After coming in contact with the enemy, had our officers and men known that Jackson and Longstreet with Hill were so near, that knowledge would have inspired them with as much courage to enter into the work before them as a reinforcement of thousands of men. Then, instead of two little guns, we ought to have brought up two full batteries and the Infantry filed off to the right and joined to Longstreet's line. I have no right, and do not mean, to criticize any one. It seems to me now that a numerous staff was needed to keep the Commanding General posted as to the movements of the different columns and to keep the Commanders of the different columns informed of the movements of each other, to ensure cooperation. Huger's Division remained in that position during the night and started early next morning. The Federal Army had moved during the night. We soon reached the position evacuated by them, passing on the road dead and wounded soldiers, articles of equipment, including some breastplates. We soon passed a battery of captured guns, as our position the afternoon before was not over two miles from the scene of Longstreet's and A. P. Hill's battle. The weather was very hot, it was July 1st, by noon we arrived at Malvern Hill and formed line of battle under the northern slope of that hill; occasionally a shell passed over our heads. The 6th Virginia was leading the Brigade and, as I was acting Adjutant, I was near the head of the column. Between two and three o'clock Gen.

Magruder came to the right of the line, where came also Generals Mahone, Armstead and Ransom. General Magruder wore a straw hat and appeared to be warm, but was lively and vigorous and gave his orders to the Generals with a clear, firm voice. "General Mahone's Brigade will form on the right, General Armstead's the center, and General R. Ransom's the left, and charge the enemy's position." General Mahone then led the way and the Brigade filed along the west side of the hill. As we ascended we saw the valley to our right, it had been sowed in wheat, which had been cut and the shucks of wheat stacked at regular intervals, which sheltered the enemy's skirmishers, who, seeing our advance, began to fire on us. I was near General Mahone when he took his binocular and examined the field and spoke of seeing the skirmishers. When the head of the column reached the summit Lieut. Col. Williamson gave the command, "On the right, by file, into line." The first three Companies executed the movement, advanced the proper distance, and laid down, for at that moment the Federal Batteries, some five or six hundred yards in front, opened a furious fire. We could not see where the rest of the 6th Regiment went, a part of the 16th Virginia took position a little to our right. Lieut. Col. Williamson did not give, in my hearing, any order to advance, but I believe he went ahead himself. We could see the Federal Batteries' over sixty guns in front, and we could see the troops on each side near us, but undulations of the ground and the growth of the high weeds and bushes prevented us from seeing where our other Companies had gone. The first three Companies, having obeyed the order given, lay there awaiting further orders. I insisted to them, and to the 16th Virginia, that I thought we should charge the Federal Battery, but I had no authority, and no one seemed to agree with me. So there we lay until nine o'clock at night, under that terrific cannonading. Some of the shells came from the Gunboats lying in the James River, which was in sight. A man was shot alongside of me. I saw Armstead's Brigade advance to our left, remember distinctly seeing the 9th Virginia advancing in line. Adjutant J. A. Crocker was in front with his sword raised—their loss was considerable, Crocker himself being wounded. They were soon out of sight. The charge was a brilliant one, but was a failure, for our troops were repulsed, and our loss in officers and men was very large. After dusk we could see the shots fired by the Federal Infantry; they looked like fireflies. About nine o'clock Captain Carter Williams assumed command of that portion of the 6th Virginia and marched it off the hill, about five hundreds yards, to a barn in the field, where we had first formed. I slept near Charles McCourt of Company "G" and Private Smith of Wilbern's Company, both of whom were shot in the breast. The ball went clear through McCourt, but he survived. Smith's wound was not serious. While ascending the hill, Wm. McLane and David Myrick were both shot in the knee—they died in a few days. They were members of Company "G." It rained hard that night and the next day. The Federal Army repulsed the attack of the Confederate Army, and inflicted upon it a heavy loss, but had also sustained a serious loss, and retreated during the night to Harrison's Landing on the James River. Our Division remained near Malvern Hill a few days, then proceeded to the south side of the James River and encamped near Falling Creek. While at that Camp Regimental Commanders were directed to select each three Lieutenants to go in search of men who had been assigned from the Militia while at Norfolk to different Regiments, had been taken sick while there, and at the evacuation of that part of the State, were permitted to go to their homes, promising to return as soon as they were able. Lieutenants Crawley, Happer and myself were detailed from the 6th Virginia and ordered to proceed to Franklin and Patrick Counties. General Huger was relieved from Command of the Division and General R. H. Anderson was sent in his place.

Chapter 3

March to Winchester

It was late in July when the three Lieutenants arrived at Rocky Mount, the County seat of Franklin. We had great difficulty in finding the absentees, as they were scattered in different parts of that mountainous country and would hide in the thickets. They had very little relish for service in the Army. Most of the good men of that section had volunteered at the beginning of the War. These whom we sought had been drafted when the Militia was called out. After seeing a few and directing them to report on a certain day at the railroad depot at Big Lick, twenty-eight miles from Rocky Mount, I was selected to meet and conduct them to Richmond. I went to the depot; not one of them appeared. We had no means of taking care of them, hence had to rely on their promise to report. I returned to Rocky Mount. That little village was then quite inaccessible, the roads leading to it were bad, and it was considered a good point for refugees from the theater of the War. Ex-Governor Henry A. Wise had rented a commodious and comfortable house there for his family, while he commanded a Brigade in the western part of the State. His sons, Henry A. and John S., then young, were there. The former, as a student of Divinity; the latter, a youth of about sixteen, spent a good deal of his time at our quarters. We found him very agreeable and interesting. Hughes Dillard, a prominent lawyer, lived in a very pretty cottage on the main street opposite to our quarters. John S. Wise knew the family very well and invited me to go with him to make a call. I accepted and found Mr. Dillard, his wife, and three daughters, very charming people. The young ladies were Miss Bettie, Miss Mattie, and Miss Pattie. There were also three young sons. Miss Mattie pleased me very much and when they left one morning early for Henry County, where they intended to spend the balance of the season, I found Rocky Mount a rather lonesome place. About that time also came the news of Jackson's movement against Pope's Army in Culpepper County and then the evacuation of the James River Peninsula by McClellan's Army, and I determined to apply for an order to return to my Regiment. The request was granted and I bid adieu to my two comrades, and set out for Richmond. By the same conveyance John S. Wise left to enter as a cadet at the Virginia Military Institute at Lexington, Va.

I arrived in due time at Richmond and, after making some necessary purchases, I took the railroad train for Rapidan Station on the road to Alexandria. We arrived in the afternoon. The railroad from that point to Manassas was not in running order. The two Armies had been disputing for its use and it was badly torn up. General Lee's Army, after driving Pope's Army back to the entrenchment near Washington, had crossed the Potomac and was in Maryland. An order was issued for officers and men returning to the Army of General Lee, then known as the Army of Northern Virginia, to proceed to Winchester and await further orders. I left my valise with other baggage piled there on the bank of the river, and drew rations, consisting of raw bacon, cooked lamb, and bread. When I met Lieut. Lewis White, of the Cavalry, as we had to walk to Winchester about seventy miles, he proposed that we should make the journey together. I accepted and found him a very agreeable companion. It took us four days to make the march. The first day we walked along the railroad to Culpepper Court House, meeting on the way a good many Federal prisoners, some with red Zouave trousers. It seemed very queer, we passed close to them, neither side made any remarks. We learned afterwards that they were permitted to go that way as prisoners under parole to report themselves to the authorities at Richmond. Sometimes we would find Army wagons going in our direction and would get them to carry us a few miles. At night we stopped with friendly country people. We crossed the Blue Ridge at Chester Gap and spent one night at Front Royal. On the fourth afternoon we arrived at Parkin's Mill, five miles from Winchester, about the 10th of September. There were several attractive young ladies at the Parkin's House. After resting, I wished to push on to Winchester, but I could not induce my companion to leave Parkin's Mill, so I went alone to our destination and never saw my traveling companion any more until after the close of the War. Since then we have been very good friends. He was and still is a very fine fellow, and a worthy citizen of Norfolk.

Chapter 4

Sharpsburg

Arriving at dusk, I felt very forlorn in Winchester, but succeeded in finding a very nice boarding house just above Taylor's Hotel, where I remained until the morning of the 16th, when an order was published for officers and men to push on towards Harper's Ferry and join their Commands. Lieut. Col. Williamson came to the boarding house while I was there, so on the morning of the 16th we set out for the Army. We found the 6th Virginia near Hall Town within a few miles of Harper's Ferry, about half past five in the afternoon. Captain John R. Ludlow was in command. Lieut. Col. Williamson assumed command and before darkness came on, the Brigade was marched off towards Sheppardstown. The road was narrow, the country wooded, and the night very dark. Col. Williamson tied a white handkerchief, so that it would hang below his neck, to guide the column, but he lost his way, or fell out from fatigue, I do not know which. The column arrived at daylight near Sheppardstown and, after a short rest, was put in motion for the ford, by which it crossed the Potomac. Adjutant-General Robertson Taylor, of the Brigade, offered to take me over the river behind him. I accepted and thus got across without getting wet. We had very little idea of where the rest of the Army of Northern Virginia was, and no idea at all as to the whereabouts of the Army of the Potomac, then commanded again by General McClellan.

We knew that Harper's Ferry had been captured on the 15th, so after reaching the Maryland shore, and hearing two cannon shots, I realized that we were approaching a field of battle, and I said to myself, "Goodness, are we going to fight a battle here with our backs to this river?" That proved to be true, for it was the 17th day of September, 1862, and the battle of Sharpsburg had commenced. The 6th Regiment had lost quite a considerable number of its men on the Charles City Road, at the Battle of Bracket's Field, at Malvern Hill, at second Manassas, and Crampton's Gap. Many had fallen out of the ranks during the night from fatigue and sore feet, so when we halted in the rear of the town of Sharpsburg, in a field on the north side of the main street, the Brigade mustered only eighty-two officers and men. General Mahone had been wounded at Second Manassas and the Brigade was commanded by Lieut. Col. Parham of the 41st Regiment. Captain Ludlow was the senior officer present with the 6th Virginia. Captain Charles W. Wilson was present and many other officers, including Lieut. Duncan Robertson and myself. The proportion of officers was entirely too large for the number of men bearing muskets. Pryor's Brigade was with us, but it also was very much reduced in numbers. After resting about one-half an hour General Pryor rode up and assumed command and ordered the column forward. It passed to the west of Sharpsburg and advanced across the fields towards Piper's farm. As soon as this body of about three hundred troops was seen by the Federals, a tremendous fire of artillery was directed against it. It proceeded by file at double quick step, crossed the Hagerstown Turnpike about one-half a mile south of the Dunker Church, entered Piper's field and stopped at the west side of a large apple orchard, but had been almost scattered by the heavy fire. I estimated that it was nearly ten o'clock A.M. There were but few of Mahone's Brigade to be seen. Lieut. Duncan Robertson was wounded while we were near Piper's barn. He was alongside of me; I stopped a moment, saw that he was shot in the foot, which bled profusely. I kept on; he crawled into the barn, where there were already many wounded. After resting a few moments, I went into the orchard and endeavored to rally enough of the 6th, whose uniforms I recognized, to form a small squad to push farther, the front line of battle was just ahead, lying in the sunken road, now called Bloody Lane. While doing so, Lieut. Col. Parham beckoned me to come to him. I did so; he said, "Lieutenant, go back a little, try and find General R. H. Anderson, explain to him the situation and ask for reinforcements." I turned towards Hagerstown Turnpike and on reaching it I asked an officer the whereabouts of General Anderson. He replied he had been wounded. I looked then towards the front and saw our troops falling back; they were coming across the field and down Piper's Lane. The officers present then commenced to rally the men and I joined them. I did not see any of our men of the 6th Virginia, all were strangers, but a line was formed along the Turnpike. Not very formidable at first, but was strengthened from moment to moment. Asking a young soldier to stop, he replied, "I have been shot in the hand." I said, "We must whip them today. Give me your gun, I will load it." I was thinking how near our lines were to the Potomac River. I took his musket and loaded it and as I returned it to him, he was wounded again, and he reproached me, saying, "Ah, if you had not stopped me." There was a confused crowd at that place, opposite to the entrance to Piper's Lane, but the efforts of the officers succeeded in forming a line along the eastern side of the Turnpike; different commands were mixed. I did not recognize there any of the 6th Virginia. Looking down the Turnpike I saw a gun standing on one side. There was no soldier with it and but one horse hitched to the limber and wounded besides. I requested the assistance of four Infantry soldiers near me, and we drew the gun to the entrance of Pipe's Lane and loaded it. The enemy's skirmishers were crossing the lane near Piper's dwelling. Just at that moment Major Fairfax, of General Longstreet's staff, stopped there and dismounted. I asked him if we should fire. He said yes and I handed the lanyard to him. He pulled it and the shell went bounding down the lane by Piper's house. He mounted and rode away. Then some voices were heard saying, "Over here is the place for that gun" and several more Infantry soldiers came and the gun was drawn to the top of the next rise in the Turnpike about fifty yards. From that point could be seen the Dunker Church, and in the field in front of it were lines of the Federals advancing towards the Church. Quite a number participated in getting the gun in position and aiming it at the advancing lines. When it was fired the shell bounded along some distance in front of those lines. It was a very poor shot. After that shot the enemy's artillery was directed in that position. The Colonel of the 14th North Carolina Regiment was there, as well as other officers, and I believe they were glad to have the gun moved, for when I remarked, "This is not the proper place for it" and directed the improvised gun's crew to draw it back to the original position, no one objected. So it was taken back. In loading the gun, I discovered that there were no more friction primers in the limber chest and requested one of the crew to go to a Battery on the elevation to the left and rear of our position and ask for a supply of primers. He did so and soon returned with them. It was none too soon, for the enemy soon appeared advancing towards our position. A Regiment or small Brigade of Confederates had been advanced from the Turnpike and stationed about one hundred feet east of the same under a slight rise in the ground and some outcropping rock, and their battle flag was waved; that movement, and the appearance of the flag encouraged the rallied men; before that some appeared to be demoralized. Between the orchard and the sunken road was a corn field, the stalks being from four to six feet in height. The enemy's line appeared advancing through the corn about three hundred yards from the Turnpike. The gun was then in just the right position to oppose their line; three shots were fired and struck them where their colors were visible. Their line halted and fell back and was hidden by the corn. In a few moments they appeared again. Three more shots were fired with the same precision; again the line disappeared. Then it advanced the third time, and again it received three more shots equally as true. As the line retired the third time, a Federal soldier turned around and fired deliberately at me, and his ball struck the ground near my feet. The Battery on the eminence to our left and rear was firing, but more to our left. The line that we fired at was partly in the corn field and extended through the west side of the orchard towards Piper's farm house. Our Infantry line did not have occasion to fire. The Federal line apparently fell back to the ravine a little to their rear and remained quiet the rest of the day, so far as we could judge from our position. The gun was a smooth bore six-pounder and supposed to belong to Huger's Battery. That Battery had been heavily engaged early in the morning in the adjoining field, and had been pretty badly used by the Federal Artillery. It had not been able to take away that gun because of the great loss of horses. A movement of the Infantry was then made; the line was stretched towards the hill, where now is located the cemetery. It was quiet on that part of the line for quite a long time. General Longstreet came along the Turnpike from Sharpsburg. He stopped and asked where were the Battery horses. I told him that we had found the gun abandoned and had been working it against the enemy. He said, "Hold on to it." I noticed that he was wearing slippers. He then went towards the left. By this time two of our Company "G" of the

6th had come up and joined us, and the temporary gun detachment
had left with their Command, which I am quite sure belonged to General G. T. Anderson's Brigade from Georgia. George M. Todd and C. Hill
were the men from Company "G" who joined. That portion of the
line, where I remained with the gun, was then held by Wright's Brigade of R. H. Anderson's Division, Colonel William Gibson, of the
48th Georgia Regiment, being in command, who came to where I
was standing and spoke of the situation. It was quiet at that moment,
but no one knew when the next blow would fall. The enemy could
not be seen in front, because of the corn, and the accidents of the terrain. He asked me what I thought he ought to do. I replied, "Advance
skirmishers and have them ascertain what the enemy is doing." He ordered forward a line of skirmishers and the line met the 7th Maine
Regiment, which, as I have since seen in the Official Report, had orders to take the eminence to our left and rear, where were some stacks
of straw. They were attacked by Col. Gibson's Command, also by some
other troops nearby, and were forced to return to their place in the
Federal line with a considerable loss in killed, wounded and prisoners.
That little affair impressed upon the Federals that the Confederate line
was on the alert and ready to meet them. Towards four o'clock—I
believe—we heard sharp musketry to our right and soon a Battery
opened in front of our position, directed on the Turnpike, as I supposed, to prevent a movement of troops from our left to our right. The
musketry firing was Burnside's attack. None of the enemy's Infantry
was in sight, although our position there near Piper's was the most advanced part of our Confederate line at that stage of the battle. A little
to our left the line made an angle and ran in rear of the Dunker Church
towards the Potomac River. The shelling was very severe and lasted an
hour or more. While using a field glass examining the fields in front,
I was struck in the face—I felt as if some one had struck me with a
fist. I was losing a good deal of blood and did not know whether or
not I was badly wounded. George M. Todd accompanied me along the
Turnpike to the town of Sharpsburg, but a short distance. At the corner
of the first street we saw several Federal prisoners and asked to what
command they belonged. They replied the 7th Maine. Todd then went
back and I urged him to try and have that gun brought off. He did so
and a detachment brought the gun off after dark. Noticing a pump in

the yard of a house in the town, I went to it and bathed my wound. The flow of blood had ceased and I concluded it was not serious. At the pump was a middle-aged citizen of Sharpsburg and two soldiers. They said the Federal Infantry had advanced quite near that place a little while before, but had fallen back. I then walked on the road towards the west, passed a group of officers standing in an open space near the street, which I took to be General Lee and staff and other Generals; kept on past the town and seeing a large stack of straw in a field, went to it, stretched myself on the straw and fell asleep, and did not awake until sunrise. Then I commenced a search for the Field Hospital of Anderson's Division. I soon found it and Surgeon Thos. B. Ward dressed my wound. By that time my face was black and blue, the bridge of my nose was slightly fractured, but there was nothing serious. He applied a large piece of absorbent cotton and it was to be kept moistened with cold water. I passed that day at the Hospital. I declined to go any further to the rear, but in the afternoon I was told that all wounded men were ordered to cross the river into Virginia, so I walked to the river opposite Sheppardstown. On my way I met an acquaintance, Lieut. Thos. H. Smith, from Lexington, who told me he was on his way to report to Col. E. P. Alexander, commanding a Battalion of Artillery. I was put across the river and after wandering around the town and not being able to find any better lodging place, I laid down on the low porch of a dwelling house, and soon fell asleep. I awoke at sunrise and walked out of town and took the road to Boteler's Ford.

During the night the Army of Northern Virginia had crossed the Potomac River and were moving through the town. I did not meet any of Mahone's Brigade, but spoke to Lieut. John Vermillion, of the 9th Virginia, of Armstead's Brigade. While sitting by the side of the road my brother, Captain George Chamberlaine, A. C. S., of the 9th Virginia, came along. He was mounted and had come up with rations for the Regiment. I joined him and we proceeded in search of the Brigade wagon train, but did not find it until the next day. We rode the horse turn by turn, and at night slept in the woods. Early the next morning we arrived at the little town called Charlestown, got breakfast at a private house and soon afterwards found the wagon train and went with it to where the Army was bivouacked on the Opequon River. Here many men who had fallen out of ranks from fatigue or

illness rejoined and our Company "G" mustered ten or twelve men.
I soon recovered from my wound and participated in the daily drills.
No other Company officer was present. After a few days the Army was
put in motion and marched to Stephenson's Depot, six miles north
of Winchester, where it remained until October 31st, then marched
to Culpepper Court House. After halting that afternoon, we had the
customary muster October 31st, which was supposed to be held every
two months. On the march from the Opequon River to Stephenson's
Depot I was detailed to command the Rear Guard. The main duty
of the Rear Guard on such a march, not in presence of the enemy,
is to keep the stragglers from dropping to the rear. It was a very hard
task, but by close attention we prevented that evil on that day. When a
column passes a spring or well, so many men rush to get water, some
with a string of canteens around the neck to get water for their comrades. The Rear Guard had to wait until all were supplied and then
catch up with the column. On arriving at the bivouack, entirely worn
out, I dismissed the Guard to their respective companies. Next morning I was summoned to Brigade Headquarters; General Richard B. Garnett had been placed in command, and asked why I had not kept the
Guard on duty all night. General Garnett was an amiable man and excellent officer. On my replying that I was not aware that the duty continued after the day's march was concluded, he said, "Very well, but
another time you must remember that." I had not received any instructions of that kind from the Adjutant-General. I presume he thought I
ought to have known. All passed very amicably and I always remem-
bered that lesson. We remained in Camp near Culpepper Court House
several weeks. It became very cold. At this time the troops were seg-
regated; Brigades were formed of Regiments from the same States, that
before were composed of Regiments from different States. General Mahone returned for duty. Our field officers also returned to duty and
many of the men. I was called on to act as Adjutant at Dress Parade and
we had again four or five hundred men in ranks. About the middle of
November the Division was ordered to march to Fredericksburg. The
Adjutant being absent, I was again called on to take his place, and rode
his horse on the march and messed at Regimental Headquarters. The
first night we halted just after crossing the Rapidan River at Raccoon
Ford. The night was dark and it rained.

Colonel Rogers had a servant who attended to the horses and Major Taylor had one who cooked. On the Colonel's spare horse was carried a large piece of canvass, which was used for making a shelter. Three fence rails were placed on end and the three upper ends tied together as a frame and the canvass hung, around it, like an Indian Tepee. The sabers and pistols were hung to one end of a rail. In the middle of the night the wind blew the tent down and the mass of sabers and pistols fell directly on my chest. It proved to be quite a shock to be awakened in that way, but no material damage resulted, and the tent was soon put up. Next day we marched to a camping place beyond Salem Church, not far from Fredericksburg. Winter was approaching and the ground was covered with snow. The turn came for the 6th to do picket duty along the Rappahannock River above the town. It marched to the cemetery above the city about dusk and relieved the Regiment on duty. Only the narrow river separated us from the pickets of the Federal Army. The weather was cold with the snow on the ground, but each one found some improvised shelter. Luckily there was no picket firing. The officers of Company "G" established themselves in a little house of one room which had been used as an office for a mill. The time of duty ended and we marched back to camp at dusk, as many troops as a Regiment, if seen by the enemy would have drawn the fire of a battery. Most of the inhabitants of Fredericksburg were still in their dwellings, but the bridge was destroyed and there was no communication. While on picket we sent one of our number into the town in search of food. He obtained a pot of preserves. During the few weeks we were in that Camp, a circular was distributed inviting young men to appear before a Board to be examined to ascertain their fitness for appointment as Artillery officers for duty with the Ordnance Corps. Richard Walke and I discussed the proposition and concluded to study the Ordnance Manual and appear before the Board. The time fixed for the examination was early in December and the place—a camp near the headquarters of General R. E. Lee on the road to Hamilton's Crossing. We reported to Lieut. Col. Broun and stood the examination. Richard Walke was the First Sergeant of Company "G." A few months afterwards he was appointed First Lieut. of Artillery for Ordnance duty, and ordered to duty on the staff of Brigadier-General Mahone. I never heard officially about my case until long after the close of the War, when I saw an official paper from the Adjutant and Inspector-General's office, giving my name among those who passed the examination and were recommended for appointment as Second Lieutenants of Artillery for Ordnance duty. I had some friends in the Ordnance Corps. Among them John S. Tucker, who lost an arm at the battle of Corinth, Miss., who was appointed First Lieutenant and afterwards promoted to a Captaincy, and Fred S. Colston, a Lieutenant and others. In the meantime a more agreeable duty was offered me.

Chapter 5

Fredericksburg

Early on the morning of the 11th of December, 1862, I was awakened by the Long Roll. The Brigade was marched to the front and took its position on Taylor's Hill a little to the left of Marye's Heights. The Federal Army, under General Burnside, succeeded in laying several pontoon bridges across the river. This work occupied most of the day, as the Brigade of General Barksdale of the Confederates contested the laying of the bridges with the engineers and their supports. The next day the Federal Army of the Potomac marched across the bridges with bands playing and colors flying and established a line extending from Falmouth along the south bank of the Rappahannock River to Massaponax Creek. During that day our Brigade was exposed to a heavy fire of Artillery. I was assigned to the command of two Companies, whose officers were absent. A man belonging to one of the Companies returned to the Command that day and as he came up to us a part of a shell cut off his canteen which hung from his shoulder. As the troops were covered by the slope of the hill, very little damage was done. Being quite unwell, I was permitted to go to the camp that night. The main battle occurred the next day, but no attack was made on Taylor's Hill and Mahone's Brigade was not called into action. The main assaults were made on Marye's Heights, a short distance to our right, and at Hamilton's Crossing. The Federal Army was repulsed with great slaughter, and after remaining one day in their position near the bank of the river, recrossed and took a position on the north side, as before the battle. The Light Battery, commanded by Captain Frank Huger, was in position on Taylor's Hill and was a part of General Mahone's Command. Upon the application of Captain Huger to the General for an officer from the Infantry, to take the place of an of-

ficer absent—sick—I was detailed for the duty and ordered to report
to Captain Huger for service with the Field Artillery. I found Captain
Huger to be an amiable man, a fine officer, and he received me as if
I had been his brother. He had two horses and allowed me the use of
one of them. The Federal Batteries were in position across the river
and at the least sight of activity on our side, they seemed to have the
lanyard in hand and the guns aimed, and a shell would come hurtling
towards our position. This was especially the case with Benjamin's Battery of twenty-pounder Parrot guns, at that time the most formidable
Field Artillery in use. We remained in position until the latter part of
December, at which time the greater part of the Artillery was ordered
back about twenty-five miles, to go into winter quarters. We had the
pine forests as a protection against the winter blasts and were near the
railroad, "Ruther Glen Station."

If I may be permitted to comment on the last two battles, I would
say that I regarded the battle of Sharpsburg at that time, as a drawn
battle. Our line, as originally formed, was forced back in some places a
few hundred yards, but the new positions were held against all assaults.
That angle of the line near the Bloody Lane and Hagerstown Pike was
never given up. Our Army remained in position all of the 18th awaiting an attack, and crossed the Potomac that night and when the Federal Commander sent the 5th Army Corps in pursuit, that portion of
it which crossed the river was driven back with considerable loss, but
after the Confederate Army returned to Virginia the Federals claimed
that it was a victory for them. It appears that A. Lincoln, the President
of the North, had made a vow that as soon as the Army of the Potomac should gain a victory that he would issue a proclamation de-
claring the slaves in the Southern States to be free, and claiming the
battle of Sharpsburg, or Antietam as they called it, to be a victory for
the Federal Army, he soon afterwards issued such a proclamation, and
it has been made good by subsequent events. But whether it was a
victory for the South or the North, the question remains, What good
did the South derive from the stand its Army made at Sharpsburg? The
Confederate Army had been in Maryland long enough to receive all
Marylanders who wished to join its ranks, and at a time when its pres-
tige was at its height. But very few joined; in fact, nearly all the men in
Maryland who wished to take sides with the South had already done

so. Harper's Ferry with its garrison and large quantities of stores of all kinds, cannon and small arms, had been captured. What else was there to be gained by remaining on Maryland soil? With the Army reduced as it was by casualties before Richmond, Cedar Mountain, Second Manassas and Chantilly or Ox Hill, and an immense number of stragglers, who had been unable for different reasons to keep up with the column and were mostly in that part of the State bounded by the Blue Ridge Mountains and the Opequon River, it seems hardly reasonable that it could do any more than hold its ground against the concentrated Federal Army of the Potomac, with its reinforcements. For these reasons it seems that it would have been better to have concentrated the Confederate Army near Charlestown. After the battle of Boonesboro, Longstreet and D. H. Hill fell back to Sharpsburg about eight miles. They were drawn up in line at that position all of the 15th and 16th of September. The Federal Army was approaching slowly. There was a skirmish on our extreme left in the evening of the 16th. That portion of the Confederate Army could have crossed without molestation on the night of the 15th and reached Charlestown on the 16th, would have met General Jackson at or near Charlestown, also the Divisions of McLaws, Anderson, Walker and A. P. Hill. As it was, the troops of General Jackson, McLaws, Anderson, Walker and A. P. Hill had to march twelve miles and ford the Potomac to join Longstreet and D. H. Hill at Sharpsburg. Some of the columns had two rivers to cross. It is within bounds to say that the Confederate Army would have been reinforced by twenty thousand stragglers had it concentrated at Charlestown. These men were able and willing to fight when in line, but foot sore and weary, they were unable to march and keep up with the moving columns. On the 17th of September, 1862, at the battle of Sharpsburg, it is stated that General R. E. Lee's Army had in line only 37,000 men. McClellan's Federal Army of the Potomac was fully twice as strong in numbers. That the Confederates withstood that host and held their ground is wonderful. The battle cost the Confederates some of its best officers and over ten thousand men, and then the slaves were freed on the strength of what President Lincoln regarded as a victory. Had the Confederate Army concentrated at Charlestown perhaps there would not have been any battle before the one at Fredericksburg. At the latter place our ardor was somewhat cooled and the Army was drawn up in a fine defensive position. Our losses were comparatively small and the loss inflicted on the enemy was very great. Like the Confederate Army, after the battle of Sharpsburg, the Federal Army remained one day on their original battle line, but they were protected by the batteries placed on the north side, where the banks are high and dominate the low lands on the south side. It is not always practicable to remain on the defensive, which was demonstrated at the battle of Chancellorsville, which occurred some four months later. There tactics of an entirely different character were necessary and our Commander-General R. E. Lee displayed his military talent in the most conspicuous manner. But let us see what happened to the writer who is simply giving his personal recollections and risking occasionally a comment on the general movements.

Chapter 6

Field Artillery

Soon after being established in quarters for the winter, all of the Artillery was ordered to the front, because of a movement made by General Burnside. He threatened to cross the Rappahannock River at Banks Ford, six miles above the old position and at other fords. We marched over the Telegraph Road towards Fredericksburg and were sent to Banks Ford. As the movement was abandoned by the Federal Commander, the Artillery was immediately ordered back to their winter quarters. The roads had become very bad, and when some twelve miles on the way back a snow storm set in. Huger's Battery was alone on the march. We bivouacked that night, and started early next morning for our winter quarters, and under ordinary circumstances should have reached there by one o'clock P. M., but owing to the mud and snow, two of our guns became stalled. There were three guns. Captain Huger went with the first and got through to the quarters by sunset. Lieut. Gale had one gun, and I the third. Lieut. Gale's gun was stalled; the road was narrow with quite a bank on each side. The third gun could not pass, the weather was intensely cold, the cannoneers had walked on, so we were compelled to leave the two guns at a point about five miles from the winter camp. We rode on, reported the trouble to Captain Huger; night had come on, so he sent men and horses for them early next morning, and the guns were brought in. The men had built huts for themselves and managed to keep fairly comfortable; the officers had tents, and the horses provided with shelter of small pine trees cut down and placed in the form of sheds. With plenty of pine straw and the adjacent pine thickets, they fared very well. There was a long line of batteries there; among them the Companies of the Washington Artillery, Bearing's Battery, the Blues from Norfolk, and many others.

The Washington Artillery men improvised a theater and we enjoyed the performances and the songs. It was a fine place for winter quarters, not hilly and dry, with a running stream nearby. I thoroughly enjoyed the two months spent there. In the latter part of February, I received an order from the Headquarters of the Army, through the regular channel, to report to Colonel S. Crutchfield for duty as Adjutant of the Artillery of the 2nd Corps. Huger's Battery was attached to the 1st Corps, commanded by Lieut. General Longstreet. The 2nd Corps was commanded by Lieut. General Jackson (Stonewall) and Col. Crutchfield was then the Chief of Artillery of Jackson's Corps.

Chapter 7

Service on the Artillery Staff

The Artillery of the 2nd Corps was then in winter quarters near Milford Depot and consisted of six battalions commanded by Col. J. T. Brown, Majors H. P. Jones, Thomas Carter, Lieut. Col. R. L. Walker, Major R. Snowden Andrews, and General W. W. Pendleton, Chief of Artillery of the Army of Northern Virginia, commanded all the Artillery of that Army then in winter quarters, with headquarters some ten miles distant and near Hanover Junction. The reorganization of the Artillery had been achieved during the winter; that is, instead of having one battery assigned to each Brigade of Infantry, it was organized into battalions of from four to six batteries, each battalion commanded by a Field Officer. When the Army started on a campaign one battalion was ordered to report to each Division Commander, to be under his immediate supervision in battle, and the other battalions remained under the command of the Chief of Artillery of the Corps to which it belonged, and constituted the Reserve Artillery of the Corps, and on its arrival on the battlefield received its orders from the Corps Commander. The Chief of Artillery of the Corps had a staff consisting of Adjutant, afterwards Adjutant-General, a Major of the Quartermaster's Department, a Major of the Commissary Department and an Ordnance Officer and the Battalions were provided for by those Supply Officers. As soon as practicable, after receiving my order, I bade my friends adieu and set out on a horse I had purchased, with my servant, a mulatto man named William Poole, for the railroad depot at Milford. I think the distance to Colonel Crutchfield's quarters was fifteen miles. When I arrived at the Mattapony River, which is a short distance from Milford Depot, I found that river very high, spreading on the south side over the causeway and woods. It was impossible for a stranger to tell where was the causeway. There were wagons and horse-men waiting, not knowing what to do. I said to them, "If there is any one here familiar with the road, I will follow him." The offer was accepted by one rider; it seemed he simply wanted company. We went along and fortunately kept on the causeway, and after proceeding some distance, saw above the flood, the upper part of the arch of the bridge over the regular channel. We crossed in safety, and after many inquiries I found the way to Colonel Crutchfield's quarters. He was established for the winter with the Battalion of Lieut. Col. Walker on the Estate of Mr. De Jarnette. It was night when I arrived there. I disposed of the servant and our horses, and accepted Col. Crutchfield's invitation to share his tent until another could be obtained. I made the acquaintance of many officers in the Artillery of the 2nd Corps, some of them attained great prominence in the Army, men of great ability and intelligence. In this Command were Colonel J. Thompson Brown, Lieut. Col. R. L. Walker, Majors H. P. Jones, Thomas M. Carter, Captains William Pegram, Carter M. Braxton, D. G. McIntosh, Thomas A. Brander, Lieutenants James Tyler, George M. Cayce, W. Gordon McCabe, Richard Byrd and J. H. Chamberlayne. We enjoyed the hospitality of the De Jarnette family, on whose estate the cantonment of Walker's Battalion was located; the other Battalions were within a radius of five miles. But the spring was approaching and active service was to be expected on any day.

On the 28th of April Colonel Crutchfield rode off to the Headquarters of General Pendleton for a conference. On the next day about 12 noon, a telegram came to our quarters from General Jackson, as follows: "Have the Artillery at Hamilton's Crossing at dawn to-morrow." I opened the telegram and went to Lieut. Col. Walker's tent and showed it to him and Captain Braxton, who was present, and after getting their advice, issued an order for the Artillery to start at once for the place designated, leaving a small guard at each Camp to look out for the sick and property which could not be sent with the batteries, and by three o'clock P. M., the last of the column was on its way. Colonel J. Thompson Brown was next in rank to Colonel Crutchfield, his headquarters were five miles distant, so the order was signed by order of Col. Crutchfield. No instruction had been given me for such an event. As the rear of the column was leaving, Col. Crutchfield appeared. He asked me why I had not turned the command over to Col. Brown. He was evidently in a bad humor. I replied that I did not think the exigency of the occasion permitted any delay. It would have taken considerable time to have turned over the command to Col. Brown and it would have been late in the evening before the command could have been gotten on their way. The telegram led me to believe that the service of the Artillery would be required at dawn, and after a march of twenty-five miles, the men and horses should have time for rest before engaging the enemy. As it was the head of the column reached Hamilton's Crossing by ten o'clock that night. When we reached that place, Col. Crutchfield went at once to report to General Jackson and sent me to announce the arrival of the Artillery to General Rodes. He had retired for the night, but his voice came to me from the inside of his tent, saying he was glad to hear it. That country around Hamilton's Crossing was new to me. I found General Rodes, but after that I had a hard time to find Col. Crutchfield, or anything else, and have no idea where I rested, but remember well I was up early the next day and rode with Col. Crutchfield along the line. A part of the Federal Army had crossed the Rappahannock River and deployed and were threatening the line extending from Hamilton's Crossing towards Fredericksburg; that was Sedgwick's Corps. The main body of the Army of the Potomac had marched up the left bank of the river, crossed at several fords, and were marching against the left flank of the Army of Northern Virginia. General Hooker had succeeded General Burnside in command of the Federal Army. Soon afterwards General Jackson's Corps was ordered to march towards our left wing. When the head of the column of Artillery reached Salem Church, on the Fredericksburg and Orange Plank Road, we found that Anderson's Division had been engaged with a part of the Federal Army, which was retiring slowly towards Chancellorsville. I was sent forward to report to General Jackson the arrival of the Artillery and told to ask him if he desired it sent forward by Battery or Battalion. I found him near the skirmish line. There was a thick copse of wood near, in which the enemy's skirmishers were supposed to be. General Jackson's reply was, "Have a battery planted there," pointing to a position commanding the woods. Almost at once a battery was placed at the point indicated. Someone else had ordered it. I started to return, when seeing a little way towards the left

Captain Huger with a section of 24-pounder Howitzers on the line, I stopped a moment to speak to him. Lieut. Col. E. P. Alexander was with him. While there I saw a shot fired at the Federal skirmish line, which brought down one man. The enemy was retiring, but to what point? That was what General Lee wished to find out, as I saw Colonel Tallcot trying to ascertain the direction the Federal skirmishers were going, whether towards Chancellorsville or the United States Ford. It turned out to be the former place. The Confederate column pushed on and in an hour or two reached the neighborhood of Chancellorsville. This was the first engagement since I had become a Staff Officer— mounted—I thought of how I should conduct myself. Capt. Braxton had once said that the position was one which often took the officer into some very hot places. I determined to ride by the side of Col. Crutch- field and keep dressed to his left as near as possible. As the column as- cended the slight hill to Chancellorsville, a Federal Battery fired on it. It had approached too near the Federal position in column. It was necessary to return. The guns and caissons were turned around—I have often thought if the enemy had discovered the true situation a charge by a squadron of Cavalry, or an advance by Infantry, could have de- stroyed the usefulness of a good many of our guns. Baron Marbot speaks of that sort of mistake in his memoirs, when the French Army pressed too closely the retreating Spaniards through a mountain pass. The French troops were too closely packed in a narrow road and were unable to defend themselves and suffered severely. Fortunately in the case in question, the country was wooded and our condition was not found out. The column turned back without damage. The Infantry was in line to the right of the Plank Road. On the left there was Cav- alry, but none in sight. Col. Crutchfield moved to the left, then en- tered a narrow road leading towards the enemy to make a reconnais- sance. We rode several hundred yards, when a battery opened on us. We turned to regain the column, galloping—the shots passing over our heads. A limb of a tree, extending over the narrow road, took off my cap. I thought to myself, what a ridiculous sight I would make if I returned without my cap; so I stopped, dismounted and recovered it. Passing on a little farther the firing ceased. Then I saw two fine rub- ber blankets left by the Federals. I picked them up and attached them to my saddle. I had purchased from the Ordnance Department a fine

English saber which I had worn for more than a year, but as it was not the custom at that time for Staff Officers to wear their swords, it was left with my baggage in the Headquarters' wagon. It was taken by someone and I never saw it again. When we returned to the Plank Road, we found the column of Infantry at a halt. Quite a brisk Artillery duel was going on a little to the right. General R. E. Lee was there. He called for General Pender commanding the leading Brigade, and I heard him say to the latter, "General, send some sharpshooters to pick off the gunners of that Battery." Very soon afterwards several Cavalry Officers rode up from the left and said one of General J. E. B. Stuart's staff named Channing just been shot a short distance from where we were standing. Night came on, the firing ceased, and Col. Crutchfield went back to the Headquarters' wagon, where we passed the night. When General Jackson's Corps left Hamilton's Crossing, General J. A. Early was left there with a force to hold in check Sedgwick's Corps, then threatening the Fredericksburg position. On the march towards Chancellorsville, we saw a balloon on the north side of the river ascend about four hundred feet, from which officers watched the movements on our side.

Chapter 8

Chancellorsville

Early next morning, May 2nd, Jackson's Corps was on the march by way of the Catherine Furnace towards the Brock Road. The Infantry had flankers, or skirmishers, out, but the road was so narrow and the woods so thick, that often the line of flankers was within a few steps of the column. Occasionally in the clear space I could see a Cavalry vidette. Col. Crutchfield rode at the head of the column with General Jackson, General J. E. B. Stuart, Major Von Bourck, Major Chew, and several other officers. When I reached the Plank Road I saw General Jackson and another officer ride along that road and stop at a turn of the same for observation. They then rode back and the column kept on the Brock Road until it reached the Old Orange Turnpike. While approaching the latter General Stuart was with the Cavalry skirmishers. They were advancing through a field covered with broom straw and bushes. The line hesitated a little, whereupon General Stuart called out to them, "Go ahead, there is nothing but Cavalry there." Finally the old turnpike was reached a little east of the Wilderness Tavern. There were woods on each side. The Infantry commenced to arrive and was at once deployed. The officers were warned not to give their orders in a loud voice. There were twelve or more officers in a group on the road, when Major Von Bourck and another officer rode towards the east to reconnoiter. They returned in a short time and reported that one had climbed a tree and had seen the enemy's position. They had two guns pointing towards the west, but the men were evidently not expecting an attack, as they were laying around smoking, some playing cards, and a little back from the road were preparing food. About that time a report came that the enemy had attacked the column on the road near the Catherine Furnace, and Col. Crutchfield dispatched several couriers at different times to the Battalions of Artillery and for the wagon train to take another road, and come to the Wilderness Tavern. It took considerable time for the Infantry to arrive and deploy. Evening was approaching and I was ordered to proceed to Wilderness Tavern and await the train. While I was there the order to advance was given, and the pursuit was so rapid that it was quite dark before I reached the front. I was not able to find Col. Crutchfield. At last I attached my horse to a tree and lay on the ground and slept until daylight. Next morning I found lying near the side of the turnpike the body of Col. Frank Mallory, of the 55th Virginia Infantry. There were many more dead Confederates. Col. Mallory was the son of a neighbor of my father and college mate of my older brother. I cut a lock of hair from his head to carry to his family. I then inquired for Col. Crutchfield and learned that he had been wounded the evening before; also General Jackson. I then went back to the hospital near the Wilderness Tavern, and as the Surgeon, Dr. McGuire, was about to operate on Col. Crutchfield's wounded leg and needed assistance, I remained and held cotton saturated with chloroform to his nose, while Surgeon McGuire removed the pieces of broken bone from his wound. The third day of the Battle of Chancellorsville was being fought at that very time. That night I slept in the Hospital Tent. General Jackson was lying wounded in the next tent and I heard one of his staff read the message of condolence from General Lee to him. One of General Jackson's couriers was lying in the tent shot in the stomach. He asked me to get him some water. I did so. When we awoke next morning he was dead. General Jackson was then placed in an ambulance and sent to Guinney's Station, and Col. Crutchfield was sent to his father's farm in Spottsylvania County, about twenty miles distant. He left his horse in my care. General Jackson died in about one week. Col. Crutchfield was disabled for eighteen months and never returned to his position as Chief of Artillery of the 2nd Corps. The Battle of Chancellorsville was over when I rode to the front and reported to Col. J. T. Brown, who said he would be glad to have me remain at his Headquarters, but he had his own Adjutant, who was Venable, his brother-in-law. Lieut. Col. R. L. Walker was present at the interview and said he would like to have me accompany him, which was agreed to. The Army returned to its old position near Fredericksburg and was organized into three

Corps. Many promotions were made. The 1st Corps was slightly reduced in numbers. Lieut. General Longstreet remained in command. Major Generals B. S. Ewell and A. P. Hill were made Lieutenant Generals, and assigned to the command of the 2nd and 3rd Corps, respectively. Lieut. Col. Walker was made Colonel and Chief of Artillery of the 3rd Corps. Colonel A. L. Long was made a Brigadier-General and Chief of Artillery of the 2nd Corps. I saw General Long soon afterwards and he told me it was the understanding that I should go with the Artillery of the 3rd Corps, which was then composed of the Battalions of Lieut. Col. Cutts, Major William Pegram, Major D. G. McIntosh, Major W. A. Poague, and Lieut. Col. John J. Garnett. This Artillery command proceeded to a Camp near Guinney's Station, and made preparations for the next campaign. I rode to see Col. Crutchfield, who was confined to his bed, but gradually improving. While at this Camp, news was received of the death of Gen. T. J. Jackson, Commander of the 2nd Corps Army of Northern Virginia, and the Rev. Dr. Moore, of Richmond, repeated his funeral oration of General Jackson at a church near our Camp, which we heard. It was sublime; an inspiration to the soldiers to follow his example of devotion to duty in the Southern cause.

Chapter 9

Artillery of the Third Corps

Early in the month of June the command was ordered to march to Fredericksburg. The Artillery of the 3rd Corps was by that time thoroughly organized. Our Quartermaster, Major Wm. C. Scott, was a very efficient officer and the command was provided for in every respect except we lacked a supply of horse shoes. We had a small corps of couriers detailed from different batteries, who were intelligent men. A young man named J. W. League from Smithfield, one of the couriers, was used as a clerk in the Adjutant's office. Charles H. Buskey, of Norfolk, was courier and also a Mr. Bragg, from Orange County. On our arrival at Fredericksburg, we found the Infantry of the 3rd Corps, R. H. Anderson's Division, H. Heth's and C. M. Wilcox's Divisions, confronting a force of General Hooker's Federal Army, which had crossed the pontoon bridges to the south side of the river, and appeared to have the intention to attack. General A. P. Hill's field headquarters were on Howison's Hill. The Corps of General Longstreet and Ewell were at Culpepper Court House, about forty miles to the west. General Lee was about to invade the State of Pennsylvania. The main body of the Federal Army was near Falmouth, and General Hooker was trying to ascertain the intentions of General Lee. The former sent a large force of Cavalry to Brandy Station, accompanied by two Brigades of Infantry to reconnoiter. The result was a severe Cavalry battle which lasted all day, when the Federal forces retired. They discovered a part of the Confederate Infantry near Brandy Station. The force that was in front of General A. P. Hill then recrossed the river. The next day the 3rd Corps marched in the direction of Culpepper Court House. We passed by Chancellorsville where six weeks before had been fought that bloody battle. We saw the strong entrenchments which Hooker's Army had thrown up just in the rear of that place. We crossed the Rapidan River at Ely's Ford and reached Culpepper Court House early on the third day. Next day the Artillery marched to Sperryville, the Infantry took a shorter route by Gaine's Cross Roads. We pursued the route via Front Royal and arrived at a place near Berryville where we remained in camp during the 21st and 22nd of June. I was engaged at that place in making the Field Report of the Artillery of the 3rd Corps. As well as I can remember, we had eighty odd guns and fifteen hundred men, with a full compliment of horses and wagons, besides the Ordnance Train under Captain L. Points, with Lieut. Henry Thorburn acting quartermaster. It was understood at that time that the Army of Northern Virginia consisted of three Corps of three divisions each, and the divisions had six thousand men for duty. General J. E. B. Stuart commanded the Cavalry, with its Horse Artillery. The Artillery of each Corps had eighty odd guns and about fifteen hundred men. On the 23rd of June we started on the march for Pennsylvania, bivouacked near Sheppardstown, crossed the Potomac River the next day, and marched to Hagerstown. There we found Longstreet's Corps passing through that town. The night we spent at Sheppardstown I went with Col. Walker to the house of the Hon. Mr. Boteler and spent part of the evening. General Archer was there and Lieut. Lemon of his staff. Leaving Hagerstown next morning we took the eastern road by Waynesboro, camped at Fayetteville. On the march the Artillery accompanied General Pender's Division. We remained at Fayetteville several days and on the 30th started for Cashtown, passing through the Gap near which was located Thad. Stevens' Furnace. We passed General R. E. Lee standing near the road in full uniform with sword belt, but no sword. To us young men he had the appearance of being in fighting humor. While we were marching towards Fayetteville, our Colonel dispatched Lieut. J. H. Chamberlayne and several enlisted men to get horses. They crossed the mountains to the east, but did not return; they were captured. As we were descending the mountain near Cashtown, there was a sudden halt of the column of wagons in front of us. That usually indicates that the enemy has been seen. It turned out to be Pettigrew's Brigade which was returning from Gettysburg. Heth's Division had crossed the mountain the day before and stopped at Cashtown. On the 30th General Heth sent Pettigrew's Brigade to Gettysburg, eight miles southeast, to obtain a supply of shoes. They discovered that Gettysburg was occupied by the enemy, therefore abandoned the plan of getting shoes and returned. That Brigade was just returning to Cashtown when Pender's Division arrived in sight, hence the sudden halt of the column. Soon afterwards we reached the outskirts of Cashtown and bivouacked for the night. General A. P. Hill that night determined to make a reconnaissance in force the next day to ascertain what was in front.

Chapter 10

Battle of Gettysburg

When General A. P. Hill started his column across the mountain on the 29th his orders were to proceed through Gettysburg towards York. Ascertaining from General Pettigrew that the enemy occupied Gettysburg, as became the able soldier that he was, he notified General Lee and General Ewell and proceeded early on the morning of July 1st to make the reconnaissance, sending forward Heth's Division with Pegram's Battalion of Artillery, followed by Pender's Division and McIntosh's Battalion of Artillery. Col. Walker rode at the head of the column with a three-inch rifle gun of Captain Edward Marye's Battery. The skirmishers were in front. When they reached the crossing of Marsh Run, the place looked suspicious, the banks of that stream were covered with trees and underbrush, so the skirmishers halted. The three-inch rifle gun was brought up and fired one shot, whereupon the Federal Cavalry skirmishers rose and retreated. That place is about four miles from Gettysburg. The column pushed on and soon arrived at Willoughby Run, two miles farther. There General Heth ordered Archer's Brigade to deploy on the right of the road and advance in line across the Run, which was done. The enemy's Cavalry had determined to make a stand there and two batteries were in position on the hill east of the Run. I have since learned they were Hall's and Calef's Batteries. Just at that time the leading Brigade of Reynold's First Corps of the Federal Army arrived on the scene and attacked that portion of Archer's Brigade which had crossed the Run, captured the General and several hundred men, while the Batteries opened fire on the troops arriving on the other side. It was then evident to General Heth with whom he had business. As the other Brigades of Heth's Division arrived they were deployed on the hill on the west side of Willoughby

Run. Lieut. John Morris had one of his legs crushed by a shell. We saw
him as he lay in a dying condition on the hill near Pegram's Batteries.
He died soon afterwards. Col. Walker then rode back towards Cashtown where the Reserve Battalions of Artillery had remained and ordered them to the front. The contest was kept up at that place for several hours from each side of the Run. Davis' Brigade crossed the Run
and attacked the right flank of the Federal First Corps at the Railroad
Cut, assisted by Captain Brander's Battery, but without success. On
Col. Walker's return to the front, we were riding near our Infantry line
on the right of the road, when one of our Infantry men brought a
Federal Cavalry soldier of a Michigan Regiment from the front, where
he had captured him. Colonel Walker received the prisoner and directed me to conduct him to General A. P. Hill, who was on the hill
just west of the Run. General Hill asked him a few questions then
turned him over to the Provost Guard. The Cavalry man was mounted
and fully equipped. I took possession of his holster in which was an
Army revolver and attached it to my saddle bow. While with General
Hill he ordered a Battery to relieve Brander's Battery, whose ammunition was exhausted, and by order of Colonel Walker, Maurin's Battery was sent to relieve Brander's. At that time, about 2:00 P. M., General Hill was watching for the arrival of Ewell's Corps, the head of
whose column could be seen near the right of the Federal line. As soon
as Ewell's troops deployed, the battle was renewed and in an hour or
two the Federal line gave way and was pursued towards Gettysburg,
Pender's Division having advanced in support of Heth's in driving the
Federal troops from Seminary Heights. About five o'clock I saw General Lee and Longstreet riding up to Seminary Heights, and also saw
Johnson's Division of Ewell's Corps arriving on the field. The Federal
troops retreated to Cemetery Heights, south of Gettysburg, and took
position there. Night came on and we lay down to rest on the side of
the Cashtown Road. Heth's and Pender's Divisions had taken position
on Seminary Heights with Pegram's and McIntosh's Battalions of Artillery. We were up by daylight next morning. As I was riding up the
slope leading to Seminary Heights, I met General Semmes riding alone.
He asked me where the battle of the day before had been fought. I
told him he was at that time on a portion of the field. He commanded
a Brigade in McLaw's Division of Longstreet's Corps and was killed

that afternoon. Farther to the right I met General Mahone riding at the head of his Brigade. He asked me, "Where is the Enemy?" I pointed towards Cemetery Heights about fourteen hundred yards to the east and said, "over there." At that time Anderson's Division, to which his Brigade belonged, was moving into position, and he said why there is musketry firing on this side, pointing to McMillan's woods, which is an extension of Seminary Heights. That was true and the leading Brigade of Anderson's Division had to skirmish and drive away some Federal troops to take up their position in the line. General Mahone was accompanied by Colonel William Gibson, whose acquaintance I had made on the field of Sharpsburg, to which he made a pleasant allusion. I told him that I was then attached to the Artillery and he said, "That is just where you ought to be." Soon afterwards I saw the Infantry of Longstreet's Corps arriving, but seemed to be awaiting orders. I think it was then between seven and eight o'clock A. M., and the day was not clear, but overcast. The field headquarters of General Lee was near the Fairfield Road, in rear of the center of the right wing and I saw him and other officers at that point later. After reconnoitering the front, it was determined to have Longstreet attack the enemy's left flank. The order to that Corps Commander was to partially envelop the enemy's left flank and move along the Emmettsburg Road. It is several miles from the Seminary, near which I saw Longstreet's Infantry arriving to the Round Top, which was believed to be the enemy's left. When Longstreet's troops arrived there, instead of finding his troops on the enemy's left flank, he found that Sickle's 3rd Corps of the Federal Army had moved forward from the prolongation of the Cemetery Ridge and had taken position on the Emmettsburg Road as far as a peach orchard, where his line made an obtuse angle with its left running along the ridge to a place called Devil's Den at the foot of the Big Round Top. The Little Round Top was in rear of Sickle's line and was occupied by some of the Signal Corps. General Longstreet's troops were deployed in front of the two sides of that angle. It was a very strong position. Its weak spot was the point of the angle and the Confederate Artillery was posted to enfilade the two fronts. All being ready, an advance of the Infantry was ordered and a bloody battle followed. Prior to that Colonel Walker received a note from General Hill conceived in the following terms: "General Longstreet is about to attack the enemy's left, watch his movements and aid him as much as possible." I took that note and showed it to each Battalion Commander and when Longstreet's attack was made the Artillery of the 3rd Corps opened fire and followed the instructions. The enemy's Artillery replied, and a cannonade was kept up for at least two hours. The Artillery lost some men and a great many horses. Pegram's Battalion's loss in horses was very great. While that battle was progressing General Hill with his staff rode along a part of his front and in rear of McLaw's Division, which by that time had passed beyond the peach orchard and was pursuing the enemy towards the prolongation of Cemetery Heights. That gallop under the Artillery fire was very exciting, but I lost my holster with the revolver. No one was struck. General Hills' staff were occupied in rallying some of the Confederates, who were falling back in groups of two or three. I could see the Little Round Top very plainly, the enemy was drawing some guns by hand on its summit. We remained near that position until nearly dusk. At that time I saw a force of Federals moving to the front in columns of companies. That day's fighting on our right closed at dark and we returned to our quarters. Longstreet's Corps and a part of Hill's had gained considerable ground, had taken all of the position to which Sickle's Corps had moved, and driven that Corps and all the reinforcements sent to its support back to the prolongation of Cemetery Heights, which they held with their left resting on Little Round Top, at the foot of which the Confederate skirmishers remained and from that point along the Devil's Den to McMillan's woods.

Next morning we were up early and I rode to the peach orchard where were lying many dead Federal soldiers, conspicuous among them Zouaves with the baggy red trousers. On the Federal side they seemed to be strengthening their defenses. I met my old Captain Huger, then promoted to Major. He said he was trying to bring Artillery to bear on the Big Round Top, which the Federals had occupied during the night. Col. Alexander was arranging many pieces of Artillery for a grand cannonade to be opened later. I was sent to our left to notify the Commanders of the Artillery Battalions that they were to advance when their Infantry supports should move forward. As I came back I saw Heth's Division lying under the crest of the hill. An old friend, John Q. Richardson, Major of a North Carolina Regiment, spoke to me and said, "I understand that we are to charge that hill," pointing to Cemetery Hill. I looked over at the hill and the position looked so formidable that I replied I did not think the rumor was true, although the order that I had just carried to the Artillery Battalion Commanders indicated that it was true. Poor fellow, he was killed shortly afterwards in the assault. I passed on down the line and soon came to Pickett's Division also lying down under the crest of the hill. General R. B. Garnett was in front of the line, with his aide-de-camp, Lieut. John S. Jones, a relative of mine. I stopped to speak to them; they were mounted. They said nothing about the charge to be made. Soon afterwards Garnett was killed. Jones was wounded but recovered. I was trying to find Colonel Walker and soon found him riding with Colonel Walton, Chief of Artillery of the First Corps; they were riding on the Fairfield Road. Occasionally a cannon ball or shell crossed the road. During that short ride the charge of the column of attack took place, and as the view was obstructed by woods, I did not see it. When we returned I passed General Lee and Lieut. Col. W. H. Taylor of his staff, riding to meet the defeated troops. A litter passed with a wounded officer, who raised himself on his elbow and saluted the General, who looked anxious and careworn, but resolute and self-possessed. After awhile the firing ceased. Our troops remained in the positions which they had taken before the fighting commenced on the second day. That night the Corps of General Ewell left their position in front of Gulp's Hill, and took position on the northern extension of Seminary Heights; that is, on the left of the 3rd Corps.

Next day, July 4th, I was sent to a point near the Seminary and saw there a battery of the Richmond Howitzers. Occasional shots were exchanged by the Artillery of the two Armies. While at that place a shell burst very near me, which indicated that both sides were on the alert. The losses of the two Armies were fearfully large, something like forty thousand. I was near a conference of high ranking Artillery officers and heard General E. P. Alexander say that we did not have left more than four rounds of ammunition to each gun. An order was issued to leave the lines at dusk and take the Fairfield Road. A rain storm set in that evening and we found the road very muddy. We passed through Fairfield in the night and arrived at the foot of Jack's Mountain at daylight. The 3rd Corps, which led the column, stopped there during that day and the 1st Corps passed. That afternoon we started following the 1st Corps and crossed the mountain at Monterey at daylight and proceeded to the town of Waynesboro, where we halted to rest. I rode during that night the horse of Colonel Crutchfield and my servant rode my own horse. It was the custom of the officers' servants to accompany the wagons on the march. Next morning, July 6th, when we halted my servant did not appear. I did not see him again until after the close of the War. He then told me, that being very much fatigued on the night of the 5th, he tied his horse to a tree and went to sleep. After the column passed he was captured. So I lost servant, horse and equipment. The 3rd Corps reached Hagerstown on the 7th. I was permitted to take the horse and equipment of the prisoner that I had conducted to General A. P. Hill during the battle of the first of July. We stopped on the outskirts of Hagerstown several days. My father's family had removed to Baltimore and I wrote to him and mailed the letter at the Post Office at Hagerstown. When the Confederate Army left that place, communication with Baltimore was re-established and the mail went forward. While at Hagerstown, I visited the family of a former rector of Christ Church, Norfolk, Virginia, who were living in that town, Mr. Parks. On the 10th the enemy were reported advancing from Boonesboro, and the Army of General Lee was ordered to take position a few miles from Hagerstown, extending from the Williamsport Road to St. James College and beyond. The 3rd Corps was in front of that College. The Federal Army moved up and established a line in front. There was a little skirmishing, but no attack was made.

It was the intention of General Lee to re-cross the Potomac River into Virginia, but that river was rendered, by frequent rains, too deep to ford, and a pontoon bridge was being built at Falling Waters, several miles in rear of our line. On the afternoon of the 13th, I was directed to see each Battalion Commander and tell him to select an intelligent officer to go at once and familiarize himself with the road leading from his position to the main road to Falling Waters. It came on to rain and by dusk was very dark, and notwithstanding the precaution taken, one battery lost its way, and had blue lights burning in their efforts to find the road. Fortunately the enemy did not seem to notice the lights, and after awhile the Artillery column got well under way. The road was narrow and muddy, badly cut up by the wheels, and crowded. I fell asleep repeatedly while riding, but at last by daybreak we reached the pontoon bridge and rode on into Virginia and biv-ouacked at Bunker Hill.

Chapter 11

Comments on the Battle of Gettysburg

Some years ago the Count de Paris, who was writing a History of the War between the Northern and Southern States, wrote to many prominent officers, asking the cause of the failure of the Confederate Army to gain the battle of Gettysburg. If he had access to the archives of the War Department, he might have found a brief, but concise, answer to his question by General R. E. Lee himself, for in a letter written by himself to President Jefferson Davis four days after the battle, to wit, July 7th, will be found in Series 1, Vol. 27, Part 2, Serial No. 44, the following:

"Mr. President—My letter of the 4th inst. will have informed you of the unsuccessful issue of our final attack on the enemy in the rear of Gettysburg—*Finding the position too strong to be carried*—and being much hindered in collecting necessary supplies for the Army, by the numerous bodies of local and other troops which watched the passes, I determined to withdraw to the west side of the mountains."

The Army of Northern Virginia in that battle was successful in everything except their final attack. On the first day the victory was complete. That portion of the Federal Army engaged was driven from the position its Commander had chosen, at least one mile, and had lost about five thousand prisoners and many small arms.

On the second day Longstreet fought a terrific battle with two divisions, aided by three Brigades of A. P. Hill; he drove back the 3rd Corps and the 5th Corps, and all the reinforcements sent to their aid, about one mile. Ewell also gained considerable ground, but could go no farther.

On the third day the final assault was not successful, and the Confederate Army fell back to the position it had assumed on the second

day. As General Lee said in his letter of July 7th, the enemy's position
was found to be too strong to be carried. General Sickle's change of
position to the front has been pronounced a mistake. In my opinion,
it proved to be the safety of the Federal Army. It is true he was driven
from it after a terrible struggle, which so exhausted Longstreet's troops
that when they approached the extension of Cemetery Heights with
the Federal left resting on Little Round Top and with that stronghold
and the crest of the extension held by the Federal troops, he was not
able to carry it. Those two hills, Gulp's on the Federal's right, and Little
Round Top on their left, might properly be called Gibraltars on a small
scale.

The Federal position on the third day, extending from Gulp's Hill
on their right, to Round Top on their left, was an exceedingly strong
position, and it was held by two lines of Infantry, in some parts three
lines, and garnished with Artillery, with the weak point partly forti-
fied with stone walls and earthworks. Such positions are rarely carried
by assaults in front, and after the failure of the assault by the column
of attack on the third day, General Lee decided that it was too strong
to be carried and determined to withdraw his Army.

Here follows what General Lee said in his Official Report of his
final attack, which is found in Series 1, Vol. 27, Part 2, Serial No. 44,
Page No. 20: "General Longstreet was delayed by a force occupying
the high rocky hill on the enemy's extreme left from which his troops
could be attacked in reverse as they advanced. His operations had been
embarrassed the day previous by the same cause, and he now deemed
it necessary to defend his flank and rear with the Divisions of Hood
and McLaws. He was therefore reinforced by Heth's Division and two
Brigades of Penders. A careful examination was made of the ground secured by Longstreet and his Batteries placed in positions, which it was
believed would enable them to silence those of the enemy. Hill's Artillery and part of Ewell's was ordered to open simultaneously, and the
assaulting column to advance under cover of the combined fire of the
three. The batteries were directed to be pushed forward as the Infantry
progressed, protect their flanks and support their attack closely.

"About 1:00 P.M., at a given signal, a heavy cannonade was opened,
and continued for about two hours, with marked effect upon the enemy.

His Batteries replied vigorously at first, but toward the close their fire slackened perceptibly, and General Longstreet ordered forward the column of attack, consisting of Pickett's and Heth's Divisions, in two lines, Pickett on the right, Wilcox's Brigade marched in rear of Pickett's right to guard that flank and Heth's was supported by Lane's and Scale's Brigades under General Trimble."

It will be seen from General Lee's report that the component parts of the column of attack are given and consisted of two Divisions of Infantry and three other Brigades, two of Pender's and one of Anderson's, in all about twelve thousand men. The assault was a brilliant one, but it could not carry, but temporarily, a small portion of the Federal line, and being attacked in front and flank, the assaulting column was forced to retire to the Confederate line with heavy loss. Pickett's Division was reduced from four thousand, five hundred men, to about fifteen hundred, and on the return to Virginia was charged with guarding about five thousand prisoners, most of whom were captured on the first day of the battle.

That battle has been called the high water mark of the Confederate States. On the march back to Virginia Lieut. Col. Taylor told me of the capture of Vicksburg and that news, together with the failure at Gettysburg, made us feel rather gloomy. My impression of the Battle of Gettysburg from what I witnessed and from reading since the official reports is, that every portion of the Army of Northern Virginia obeyed orders and accomplished all that it was in their power to do, but that Army was not strong enough to carry that formidable position defended by the Federal Army of the Potomac.

Chapter 12

Battle of Bristow Station

The Army Again on the Soil of Virginia

After resting two days at Bunker Hill, the Artillery of the 3rd Corps proceeded with the 1st Corps and the Infantry of the 3rd Corps by way of Winchester and Chester Gap to Culpepper Court House. The Artillery encamped near Cedar Mountain and remained a few days, where I was engaged in writing a report of the Campaign. The wife of our Commanding Officer came up to meet him and stayed at the farm house of Mr. Slaughter. At Bunker Hill, I occupied one side of Col. Walker's tent. One night a thief cut open the back of the tent and took my clothes, which had been folded and laid near my head, but he must have been frightened off, for I recovered them within fifty yards. So it appears that thieves break through and steal even in an Encampment of an Army. I remember also that a thief stole the dough from our cook one night, who had placed it in an oven to rise.

The 1st and 3rd Corps then moved to Orange Court House and were joined by the 2nd Corps about the first week of August, which had to go some distance up the valley, as the route through Chester Gap was occupied by the enemy. We had a good rest at Orange Court House. I met the daughters of Mrs. Bull, who lived there, and rode with Miss Mary to Montpelier, the former residence of President Madison. The enemy occupied Culpepper Court House, about fifteen miles distant, and there were frequent alarms when the troops were called to arms. Our Artillery was encamped on the road to Rapidan Station. At this camp Major Arthur Parker, C. S., reported for duty. Major Miles Seldon, Q. M., was also ordered to report to Colonel Walker, but his orders were revoked. The Army was very much strengthened by the return of wounded and sick soldiers to duty.

About the 10th of October, General Lee determined to strike a blow at the enemy, notwithstanding the fact that the 1st Corps under General Longstreet had left us and gone to reinforce the Army in Georgia commanded by General Bragg. We set out early in the morning and crossed the Rapidan at Liberty Mills and bivouacked. Our Quartermaster, Major Scott, was the son-in-law of Mr. Graves, who lived near that place and invited me to accompany him to make a visit. I did so and found Mrs. Graves a fine old lady, who had known some of my mother's relatives. We had a good supper and enjoyed the visit, returning to the column early next morning. That day the column reached a place near Sperryville. Everyone has a grain of superstition. I believe I have very little, but I could not help remarking on a flock of black birds some distance on the road to Culpepper Court House, where the column halted, and we heard that the Federal Army having learned of our flanking movement, was retiring towards Warrentown Junction. Our column started early the next morning and proceeded by a road leading to the Warrentown White Sulphur Springs, and bivouacked near the town of Warrenton. The next day we marched to New Baltimore and then turned into a road leading to Bristow Station of the O. and A. R. R. General Heth's Division was at the head of the column, followed by Anderson's Division and Wilcox's Division brought up the rear of the Infantry. Major Macintosh's Battalion accompanied Heth and the Reserve Battalions followed Wilcox. General Heth found the Fifth Federal Corps, under General G. K. Warren, passing along the side of the railroad and attacked them with two Brigades and McIntosh's Batteries. The enemy lined the railroad embankment and, as the two Brigades approached, they received a volley of musketry and the fire of batteries posted on the hill beyond, which broke them and they retreated with severe loss, leaving McIntosh's Batteries exposed and he lost five of his guns. The Reserve Artillery arrived soon after and I was sent to the front to inform General Hill of its arrival. In going to the front I passed some soldiers who had been killed and soon came to the Division of General Anderson lying in an open field just in rear of the position where McIntosh's Batteries had been captured. I inquired for General Hill and was told he had gone towards the right. Several hundred yards to the right there was woods, and followed by courier J. W. League, I rode in that direction, and, as I did so, a battery posted on the enemy's right opened; the firing was directed towards the line of Infantry, and the shell rained over our heads. We reached the woods and were thus out of sight without being struck, but the Infantry fared badly, several men of my old Company "G" of the 6th Virginia were killed and men of other Regiments, among them Lieut. T. L. Barrand of the 16th Virginia. I found General Hill not very far off and reported the arrival of the Reserve Artillery and received instructions for the night which was fast approaching. General Hill was conversing with General Ewell, whose Corps had arrived after the engagement of Heth's Brigades.

Early next morning Col. Walker was at the Headquarters of General Hill, and I heard the latter give an order for skirmishers to advance and discover what was in front. Skirmishers were sent forward and found that the enemy had left, but they managed to carry off the five guns. Then Generals Lee, Hill and Ewell rode over the field and on the hill beyond the railroad track. General Lee seemed to be dissatisfied. General Ewell had lost a leg, but he rode his horse. He was quite bald on top of his head, with gray hair on the back. His cap covered the top of his head, but left a bald place in the shape of a quarter moon. It was so noticeable that in my mind's eye I can see it now, forty-nine years after. The army remained at that place several days, engaged in destroying the O. & A. R. R. track, then marched back to the Rappahannock River. The Artillery of the 3rd Corps encamped near Brandy Station. There was a pontoon bridge near the railroad bridge and on the north side of the river an earthwork held by some Infantry of Ewell's Corps.

Chapter 13

Army Returns to Orange Court House

After being there a few days the enemy was reported advancing and the troops were called to arms. I was on the south bank of the river where we had a Battery posted about half a mile above the bridge. We saw the Federal line advancing just across the river. The Battery opened on it, but the ammunition was so inferior that not a shot reached the enemy. The order was to retire that night to the line of the Rapidan River about fifteen miles distant. As night closed I could see the battle progressing at the bridge and learned afterwards that the Federal troops captured the earthwork and some prisoners. I was separated from Colonel Walker and was not able to find him that night. The Artillery proceeded according to the order. After riding alone towards the Rapidan River through Culpepper Court House, and not finding Artillery Headquarters, I stopped on the south bank of the Robertson River, and as the night was cold, collected some wood—rails I am almost afraid to admit—made a fire and laid down for the balance of the night. Orange Court House, near the Rapidan River, was about seven miles distant. I moved off at daylight and soon fell in with Major Wm. C. Scott, our Quartermaster, and we rode into Orange Court House together. We passed a young lady on the street and Major Scott said it was Miss Taliaferro. Later that lady married Charles W. Hardy, one of my schoolmates in Norfolk—Orange Court House was her home.

Chapter 14

Mine Run

The Artillery of the 3rd Corps went into Camp near the town, with one or two Batteries posted on the river bank. It was now late in October. We made our Headquarters on the road to Rapidan Station and hostilities were not renewed until the latter part of November, when General Meade sent his Army across the river at several fords below and the Army of Northern Virginia was ordered at daylight to march to meet its old enemy. The advance of the two armies met a little east of where Mine Run crosses the roads, leading to the wilderness and thence to Chancellorsville and Fredericksburg, and a skirmish took place a little before dark. The weather was very cold. General Lee chose the position to the west of Mine Run and after dark we moved back and took position there. The next day all was quite ready to receive an attack. Some entrenchments were thrown up. The Corps of General Longstreet was still absent. The Corps of General A. P. Hill held the right. Its flank extended beyond the plank road. On the second day the enemy's sharpshooters were very active on that side and Colonel Walker rode over there and was asked to establish another Battery on the extreme right. He sent me back on the Plank Road to bring a Battery from Lieut. Col. J. J. Garnett's Battalion. Fearing the Battery might be fired at if it passed along the entrenchments in plain view, I discovered another road by which it could reach the desired position without being seen. I found Lieut. Col. Garnett and gave the orders. He selected Captain Charles R. Grandy's Battery—the Norfolk Light Artillery Blues—I guided them to the position without mishap. The Captain and many of his men were old acquaintances of mine. It turned out that General Warren had been ordered to attack that flank, but the position looked so formidable, that he advised General Meade against it. On our side the position appeared to me to be very weak, but no doubt the posting of the Battery of Captain Grandy strengthened it. The enemy not attacking, General Lee determined to attack them the next morning near that position. Early next day, I was at Antioch Church on that side, but General Stuart's Cavalry soon discovered that the enemy had left during the night. A number of officers were in the Church conversing and the subject of slavery was discussed. I heard Lieut. Col. Marshall, of General Lee's Staff, say, that if he supposed the object of the War was to uphold the right to own slaves he would resign.

The enemy was followed for some distance, but as they had a good start, our troops did not catch up with them and before night they were back across the river. They did not leave very much behind, but an ox was found all ready to be slaughtered. I heard a prisoner complain to General Lee of being abused and taunted by some of the Confederate soldiers. He mildly rebuked the latter. The Army then returned to Orange Court House. The Headquarters of the Artillery of the 3rd Corps was established in front of the home of Major Lee, near Madison Run. Mahone's Brigade of Infantry had its cantonment near the farm of our Quartermaster, Major Wm. C. Scott, on the Run. While in Camp at Major Lee's farm, Captain McMasters was assigned to duty temporarily as Inspector General on the Staff of Colonel Walker. We rested there quietly for one month. There was a grand review of the Infantry during that month, which I attended. Lieut. Richard Walke and I called on the bride of Major R. B. Taylor of the 6th Virginia, who was staying in the neighborhood. She was Miss Lelia A. Baker, an acquaintance of ours from Norfolk, Virginia. Major Scott and his estimable wife were very kind. About the first of the year, 1864, the Artillery of the 3rd Corps was ordered to move back to Lindsay's Turnout on the Virginia Central Railroad, and establish cantonments for the winter. Headquarters was fixed at Meeksville, one mile from the railroad, and Battalion Commanders were ordered to corduroy the roads leading to the railroad depot from their respective cantonments. I obtained a ten days' leave and went to Richmond and thence to Rocky Mount, Virginia, to visit Col. Dillard's family.

Longstreet's Corps returned during the winter and encamped a few miles from us. Captain McMasters was ordered back to the staff of General Field, Commanding a Division of Longstreet's Corps, and Colonel Walker was asked to name some one for appointment as Inspector General. He turned the matter over to me and I recommended Lieut. Richard Walke, then serving as Ordnance Officer on the Staff of General Mahone. There was also a vacancy in the office of Chief Surgeon of the Artillery of the 3rd Corps. At his request, I suggested Major Herbert M. Nash, Surgeon. In due time Lieut. Walke was appointed Captain and Inspector General and he and Major Nash were ordered to report for duty on the Staff of the Artillery of the 3rd Corps. After the return from the Bristow Station Campaign, I received notice of my appointment as Captain in the Adjutant and Inspector General's Department, and was ordered to remain on duty with Colonel R. L. Walker. My appointment bore the date of October 23rd, 1863. This promotion was quite a surprise to me. While near Orange Court House the Artillery Battalion of Major King was ordered from Southwestern Virginia to join the Army of Northern Virginia. One of its Batteries was known as Otey's Battery, to which belonged my old friend John H. Sharp. This Battery had been engaged in the principal battles in Southwestern Virginia and was commanded by Captain D. N. Walker. Beverly A. Tucker, now Assistant Bishop of Southern Virginia, was also a member. I rode over to see my friends and met there also Major James Y. Leigh, a Quartermaster, who was a fellow townsman. I sent to Richmond and had a tailor make over my dress uniform, which bore the new insignia of rank and had a buff colored collar and cuffs of the same material, also a service uniform consisting of a double-breasted sack coat of fine gray cloth and sky blue trousers. I had exchanged a heavy overcoat with my brother, Captain George Chamberlaine, C. S., for a fine gray cloth cape and was then provided with suitable clothes for the coming campaign. The cape was especially useful as a protection against bad weather and was much envied by other officers. On the march to Bristow Station, Captain Blackford, Engineer, said to me, "Where did you get that faultlessly fitting cape?" I managed to keep my dress uniform and cape to the end of the War, then gave the cape to my brother, who had it dyed black. The rest of my belongings were lost during the final retreat from Petersburg. At the winter cantonment near Meeksville there was a shoemaker, who made me a pair of top boots, but the price was high—seven hundred dollars in Confederate notes. That currency was then very much depreciated and people used to say that it was necessary to take a basket to hold their money, while they could bring back their purchases in their hands from the market. The depreciation of Confederate notes made me think of a scheme for having the staple cotton as a basis for the currency. The tithe tax was then in effect. My idea was, in brief, to establish large cotton warehouses at convenient but safe points, to store in them cotton received for taxes, and to pay the troops by orders on a warehouse for so many pounds of cotton, instead of Confederate notes. Those orders would have represented actual values, and the families of the soldiers would have had something to keep the wolf from their doors. The helpless condition of the families at home caused many desertions. Some of these men were tried by Court Martial and shot, and many crosses might then be seen from the road from Orange Court House to Liberty Mills, which indicated the graves of soldiers condemned by Court Martial and executed. A soldier in our Artillery Command was tried for desertion and condemned to be shot near Orange Court House. As Adjutant General of the Command, it was my duty to be present at the execution and read the orders. I made preparation on the day appointed to go to Orange Court House. Lieut. J. T. Allyn's horse was sent to meet me at the station, but when I arrived on the ground, I found that General Hill had modified the order, and I was spared the unpleasant duty. I witnessed the execution, the man died instantly, and his wife, who was present, left with the remains for Richmond. He was said to be a bounty jumper, that is, one who made a business of enlisting as a substitute, receiving the compensation and then deserting, to repeat the fraud in another part of the Army. He received little sympathy. My military duties prevented me from elaborating the scheme for a currency of cotton orders, and it never had any existence except in my mind.

The Artillery of the 3rd Corps remained in that cantonment the balance of the winter of 1863–64. We had a great deal of snow and frequent snow ball battles were engaged in between the men of different Battalions. A Battalion commanded by Major John C. Haskell with Major Reilly as second in command, had joined our Corps. One of Haskell's Batteries, Captain Lambkin, was about two miles away from the snow battlefield and Haskell's men were being driven back by the men of Pegram's Battalion, when Haskell is said to have exclaimed, "Oh, for Lambkin or night," thus imitating the Duke of Wellington, who when Napoleon's men were gaining the advantage at the Battle of Waterloo, exclaimed, "Oh, for Blucher or night." Military operations being at a standstill, I applied for a ten days' leave of absence and went to Rocky Mount, where I was married by the Rev. John Lee, of the Episcopal Church, to Miss Mattie Hughes Dillard on the 20th of April, 1864. My friend, John H. Sharp, heard of my passing the town of Liberty and hastened to join me the day of the wedding and acted as one of the groomsmen. I returned to the Command at the cantonment at the expiration of my leave, just in time for the Wilderness Campaign. The wife of Colonel Walker was at the Camp and had Miss Rose Morris visiting her. While I was absent a large box of provisions, meats, cakes, etc., arrived at the Camp for me. My fellow officers did not wait for my return, but opened the box and gave a party with the contents. What did I care? On the 2nd of May a telegram came from General Hill, ordering the Artillery of his Corps to Orange Court House. I opened the envelope and taking it to Colonel Walker's tent, where he and the ladies were talking, said "There was a sound of revelry by night, etc." quoting a part of the poem inspired by the news of the approach of Napoleon's Army to the Belgium Capital.

Chapter 15

Battle of the Wilderness

Orders were at once issued for the march and the Artillery started for the battle ground of the Wilderness. In my youth I remember hearing my grandmother Chamberlaine in relating her experiences of the War with England in 1812, say that a family should never abandon their dwelling house until the shingles commenced to fly off. I never understood exactly what she meant until the War of which I am writing came on. It was this, and I saw many instances proving the correctness of her remark, if you abandon your house it will be ruined or terribly injured by the soldiers of whichever side have access to it; whereas if the family continues to occupy it, while they may be robbed and otherwise disturbed, rarely will the house itself be destroyed. She meant by the shingles flying off, that if a battle was going on near, then it was necessary to seek temporarily a place of safety.

As our column passed Orange Court House it was awfully inspiring to see the Army of Northern Virginia—Cavalry, Artillery and Infantry—on their way to the Wilderness, about twenty miles distant. We bivouacked the first night at Vidiersville. I had been sent ahead to Gordonsville the night of the 2nd to send some dispatches to General Hill, and was made very ill by something I ate and passed a very miserable night in the telegraph office, but joined the Command next day. We left Vidiersville very early, Heth's Division in the advance, and his skirmishers encountered those of the enemy early on the morning of the 5th of May. A heavy battle was fought in the afternoon; Heth's and Wilcox's Divisions held their ground. I had been well to the front and near sunset was at Parker's Store. Capt. Grandy's Battery was at that place and the Ordnance train was arriving. A cross road comes into the Plank Road at that place from the Wilderness Tavern on the

Old Orange Turnpike, and suddenly it was rumored that a column of the enemy was advancing by that cross road. Grandy's Artillery was ordered into Battery and was ready to fire down that road. As I had just arrived from the front from that direction I was sure there could be no enemy advancing on that road and at once rode in front of the Battery and announced my belief, but the drivers of the Ordnance wagons took fright and the leading wagon, turning to the right, proceeded at a dangerously rapid rate for Ordnance wagons, followed by the rest of the train to get away from what they believed was going to be a battlefield. I tried to assure them there was no enemy near, but without success, and had to draw my saber and galloping alongside threatened to cut down the drivers unless they slackened their speed. That effort was successful, and the panic was soon over. The trees and undergrowth was so thick that only three or four guns were brought into action that afternoon. The enemy came very near getting one which had been posted on the Plank Road. The enemy's Infantry approached so near the gun, that it had to be abandoned, but was drawn off after darkness set in. Our Headquarters were established near Parker's Store. The next morning we were up at daylight and proceeded to the front. Hancock's Corps had attacked Heth's and Wilcox's Divisions and were driving them back nearly to Parker's Store, but fortunately Longstreet's Corps arrived at that moment and filing to the right and left of the Plank Road, and facing towards the front, drove the enemy back beyond the position Heth and Wilcox held the night before. While our men were falling back I saw General Lee among them, the bullets were flying by, and it seemed to me to be a very critical moment, but as I said Longstreet's Corps was arriving. After the enemy were driven back, Anderson's Division of the 3rd Corps arrived and General Lee established his field headquarters in an open space on the left of the Plank Road beyond Parker's Store, where there were several large oak trees, it was sort of an oasis in that wilderness. There were many staff officers there of the different Arms of the Service. I remember seeing the Chief Engineer of the Army. The 3rd Corps was deployed to the left of Longstreet's troops. I was directed to conduct a section of twenty-pounder parrotts towards the left. As we reached a clear space, across which one could see for one mile, we found a Battery of Artillery firing at a line of Federal skirmishers, which had emerged from the woods. On seeing me, General Hill told me to order the Battery to cease firing, as the skirmish line was disappearing. I looked across the open space in order to see, if possible, the right flank of Ewell's Corps, which was over on Old Turnpike, but could only see the woods where it was supposed to be. Wilcox's Division was filing off in that direction. On my return to where General Lee was sitting, he directed me to come to him as I was the first officer who came from the direction of the firing. He asked the cause of the firing; then if I had seen the right flank of Ewell's Corps; then if I had seen the enemy. I replied that I had seen the place where the flank of Ewell's Corps was supposed to rest, and Wilcox's Division marching in that direction; that I had seen the reflection of the sun's rays on the musket barrels of troops in front of Ewell's Corps; also told him the cause of the firing.

There was occasionally a sputtering of musketry at the front, and some musket balls dropping around. The General muttered to himself, "Those balls keep coming this way." I did not then understand what he meant, but in a very short time, it was explained. He had ordered General Longstreet to pass around to our right and attack the left flank of the Federal Army under Hancock, and as soon as that attack should take place, the Federal musket balls would be fired in a different direction. That soon happened. Anderson's Division struck the enemy's left flank and drove it to the north of the Plank Road and cleared our front as far as the Brock Road. Very soon afterwards General Longstreet at the head of Jenkins Brigade rode to the front and some of Anderson's Division, which had advanced up near the Plank Road and seeing Longstreet and Jenkins' Brigade unfortunately supposed them to be Federals; a volley fired towards them killed Jenkins and wounded Longstreet and many of the men. That accident delayed the movement. After the wounded General was removed, I saw Lieut. Col. Taylor riding from the front accompanying his brother Captain Robertson Taylor, who had been wounded in the knee. That was the same officer who had taken me across the Potomac behind him on his horse on the morning of the Battle of Sharpsburg. He was Assistant Adjutant General of Mahone's Brigade. He recovered from that wound. Lieut. Col. Taylor was on General Lee's Staff.

I then rode to the front and a short distance ahead saw an elderly Federal General wounded in the head and was propped in a sitting position with his back to a tree. His boots had been removed and he wore white socks. He was apparently badly hurt and was picking at his nose. He died soon afterwards and his body was sent by General Lee by flag of truce to the enemy's line. It was Major General Wadsworth.

Chapter 16

Spottsylvania

General R. H. Anderson was placed in command of Longstreet's Corps and General Mahone in command of Anderson's Division. The undergrowth was on fire in many places, which communicated to the trees and man. Wounded soldiers of both Armies were burned who might otherwise have recovered. Later in the afternoon another attack was made on Hancock's line at the Brock Road, but did not succeed in driving it from the entrenchments. The Artillery of the 3rd Corps did not take a very active part in that battle, owing to the woods and undergrowth, but Poague's Battalion performed good service in one of the few clear spaces. Captain Richard Walke had reported for duty and was serving as Inspector and Aide-de-Camp. He and I accompanied Colonel Walker and were generally at his side unless temporarily absent on some duty. When one of us went off on some duty, on the return, he would take place on the left of the other, thus it was the turn of the one on the right to go for the next duty. Captain Walke was a very valuable addition to the Artillery Staff and a very agreeable tent mate.

The Armies remained quiet on May 7th. On the next day the 3rd Corps followed the 1st Corps, which had moved to Spottsylvania Court House. Our command bivouacked at Shady Grove Church and early on the 9th arrived at the Court House and took position in front of the Court House buildings, that was the right of the Army. General A. P. Hill was taken sick and General Early was placed in command of the 3rd Corps. His home was very near that of Mr. Dillard. They had been opposing candidates at the election for members of the Convention. The General was a pronounced Union man. Mr. Dillard was a Secessionist. The General was elected. As soon, however, as War was de-

cided upon by the Virginia Convention, General Early threw himself
into the movement with all his spirit and kept up his antagonism to
the end of his life. Mr. Dillard was not a soldier, had passed the age and
was not fit for military duty. I was standing near the camp fire of General Mahone, where were General Early and some of his staff, I believe
it was on the 11th, when he saw me and remarked, "I hear you have
married a young lady from my County." I replied that it was true.

It was easy to recognize General Mahone's Headquarter's wagon, for
one always saw that a cow accompanied it. That General was a con-
firmed dyspeptic and a good supply of milk was necessary.

The fighting at Spottsylvania was done mainly on the left wing and
center. Some Infantry of the 3rd Corps was sent from time to time
to reinforce the left wing. When Hancock made an attack on the extreme left Captain Grandy's Battery was engaged. Hancock forced that
wing back and crossed the River Po, but did not remain long in that
advanced position, separated as he was by that river from the rest of
the Federal Army. During his forward movement, Grandy's Battery was
compelled to retire rapidly. One of my friends, Theodore A. Rogers, of
Norfolk, fell from the seat of the limber of a gun and a wheel passed
over his right leg, crushing it. He rolled himself out of the road and
remained there some hours. After Hancock's force retired he was taken
to a Hospital. That accident was most unfortunate. He suffered more
or less the rest of his life and he was past fifty years of age, when it was
found necessary to amputate the leg. But he was courageous and bore
his sufferings manfully, and up to 1910, when he died, was an active
and useful citizen of Norfolk.

On the 12th the enemy assaulted a salient angle in the line on the
left center and captured from us a large part of Johnson's Division of
the 2nd Corps and several Batteries of Artillery. The fighting at that
point lasted all day, but the enemy made but little progress. On our
wing Mahone's Brigade was advanced, and made an attack on the flank
of the attacking force. When that movement was going on I was sent
with an order to our Batteries posted along the line, to aid the movement as much as possible. The order delivered, I started a yell to en-
courage the Infantry and was galloping back towards the right, the
enemy's batteries bombarding our line of guns, when a shell burst just
to the front and left of me, enveloping myself and horse in a cloud

of smoke. I felt the horse make an unusual movement and when one hundred yards farther, I stopped, dismounted and examining the horse found he was wounded in the knee. Just then courier Bragg was approaching and I took his horse and sent him with the one I had been riding to the rear for attention. When I reached Col. Walker he was talking with General Early, the Artillery firing continued and soon we saw General Lee galloping on the road towards us. Shells were dropping in the road, but he reached us in safety. He directed General Early to have the Batteries cease firing. Col. Walker sent Captain Walke with the order and he set off in a gallop by the same road on which General Lee had come. The latter turned around and said, "Have that officer take a road nearer the rear of the line of guns, it is a safer way." But Captain Walke was beyond hearing distance, and gave the order and returned without injury. General Grant, having failed to carry our position on the left, was moving his Army towards our right. There was comparative quietness for two or three days. Grant did not seem disposed to make another trial against our line. I was quite unwell at this time. I had not removed my boots for several nights and was sent to the Hospital at Gordonsville. That Hospital was crowded with wounded and the train was ordered to proceed to Lynchburg. I was assigned to a Hospital in that city and soon felt much better, but needed a few days more to recuperate and the Surgeon permitted me to go to Rocky Mount, where I remained a few days, then returned to the Army by way of Richmond.

The Army of Northern Virginia had moved first to the North Anna River, then to Cold Harbor, and a battle had been fought there on June 3rd, which is said to have lasted less than one hour, and in which the Federal Army lost ten thousand men. The two Armies were confronting each other at Cold Harbor when I rejoined. The picket firing was very severe. I rode with Col. Walker along the line protected by a slight rise of the ground to where Major McIntosh was preparing a pit in which to sink the trail of a Napoleon Gun, with a view of firing shell to drop into the enemy's line a short distance in front, as it was reported they were constructing gradual approach works. Nothing of importance occurred for several days, when on the morning of the 13th of June it was found that the enemy had disappeared from our front. Captain Charles W. Wilson, who commanded the Battalion of

Sharpshooters of Mahone's Division, was captured at that time. Each Division had a Battalion of sharpshooters, made up of details from the different Regiments, and as soon as a Division took its place in line, its Battalion of sharpshooters covered its front as pickets.

Before setting out for the Wilderness Campaign, while we were at the winter cantonment, my younger brothers came to see me. They were cadets at the Virginia Military Institute when Norfolk was evacuated in May, 1862. Richard graduated in 1863 and joined McGregor's Battery of Horse Artillery, with which he served to the end of the War. Henry, two years younger, was not able to keep up with his class, he said because the Battalion of Cadets were sent so often to places in the southwest of Virginia to repel raids; so after the January Examinations he was discharged. He came to me, and as permission to return to the family through the lines was refused, I concluded to choose a Battery of nice young men and have him enlist in it. He was seventeen years and some months. I asked Major W. T. Poague to recommend a Battery; he advised me to take him to Captain Ward's, from Madison, Miss. So he enlisted in that Battery belonging to Poague's Battalion, where I would be able to look after his welfare. He got through the Wilderness Campaign, but his former Captain, Major Ward, was killed at Oxford on the North Anna.

Chapter 17

Siege of Petersburg

Finding Grant's Army had left our front at Cold Harbor, the Artillery of the 3rd Corps was ordered to take the road towards the James River. We crossed the Chickahominy River, passed near Bottom's Bridge and pursued the road to the crossing of White Oak Swamp. I was approaching familiar ground, but we were not expecting to meet the enemy so soon.

Col. Walker was riding with General John R. Cooke, commanding a force of Infantry, the Artillery column following. As soon as we crossed the swamp we found the enemy on the Charles City Road. General Warren's 5th Corps of the Federal Army with Cavalry was screening the movement of the rest of that Army towards the James River. Quite a brisk skirmish took place, but as night was approaching the fighting soon ceased. Next morning the enemy had left.

Our Corps remained at that place several days. Captain Walke and I rode over to Malvern Hill, about two miles distant. Having been present at that battle, we thought we would recognize the field, but we could not, the appearance of a battlefield is so much changed in two years by the growth, be it of bushes, weeds, or a different crop growing in the fields, that we were on the ground before we knew it, and then only by information from a Cavalry man, one of the force watching that flank. Perhaps if we had had more time, we might have traced the charge of Mahone's Brigade at that battle, but we were obliged to return to Camp.

On the 17th, the Corps was ordered to march to Petersburg. The first night we bivouacked at Four Mile Creek and early next morning crossed a pontoon bridge near Drewry's Bluff. Soon after crossing, we passed General Lee, who was alone. Those were exciting times;

the fact of Grant's having crossed his Army over the James River and
was marching against Petersburg had just become known to him, but
he looked as serene as a May morning. He had sent the 2nd Corps
under General Early from Cold Harbor to Lynchburg and was going
to meet General Grant again with the 1st and 3rd Corps, reinforced
by the force under General Beauregard. The latter General with his
small force had manfully resisted the first assaults of the advance of
Grant's Army, had displayed great ability in the management of his inferior force.

Our column reached Petersburg about two P. M. As we passed Bol-
lingbrooke Street, I left the column, went to Mr. Norman Page's house
for a few minutes to see my sister-in-law, Mrs. George Chamberlaine.
There was great excitement in the city, the Federal Artillery was shelling it. I found Mrs. Chamberlaine well. While there a shell struck a
house diagonally opposite and raised something like smoke. There was
no other man near and I was asked to carry a bucket of water to ex-
tinguish the fire. I took the water up to the third story; arrived there
I found the shell had not set fire to the house, but had raised much
plaster dust, which had been taken for smoke. I soon left and caught
up with the column. Mahone's old Brigade was marching up from
Pocahontas Bridge, the 12th Regiment, composed mainly of Petersburg men, at the head of the Brigade, then commanded by Col. D. A.
Weisiger, and the band was playing a lively tune.

It was a long time since that Regiment had been in Petersburg, and
oh, so many who had gone away with it were then missing, many of
them dead, killed, some by bullets, others had died of disease, and many
more were going to follow the same sorrowful road before the end of
the siege.

The 3rd Corps took position on the right and our guns were placed
in the entrenchments already happily provided for just such an event
as was then taking place. There was fighting going on at that time, but
some distance from our position. Captain Walke and I rode over to the
river above the bridges and enjoyed a swim. It was then the 18th day
of June, the weather was very warm and the roads were dusty. Artillery Headquarters were established out Halifax Street near a railroad
cut back from the dwelling houses. Occasionally a force of Infantry
was sent out in front accompanied by Artillery. One of these expedi-

tions led by General Mahone encountered the 2nd and 6th Corps of the Federal Army and took many prisoners. In this engagement the Captain of my old Company, E. M. Hardy, was wounded in the head, but recovered. The battle took place a short distance in front of our line of guns, but was not visible on account of the woods. One of our Batteries, Captain Grandy's, was placed in position on arrival in the Reeve's Salient, which was really beyond the left of our Corps, but having occupied the works there it was found next to impossible to withdraw it, because of the proximity of the enemy's earthworks; they fired at anything which appeared above our earthworks, whether it was a head or only a hat.

The Battery had to remain there for several months and had a very hard time, losing many men. Wm. E. Taylor was a Sergeant in that Battery. He obtained a furlough and was on a train which had an accident, his knee being badly injured. He is still living in Norfolk and one of its most highly esteemed citizens, but he has never recovered entirely from that injury, which often gives him a great deal of trouble. During the month of July on General Burnside's front the enemy were preparing a mine; to prevent the discovery of his work, the pickets kept up a fusillade daily. At last, on the 29th of July, it was all ready, and was exploded early on the morning of the 30th. It blew up a number of men and several guns, and his columns charged over his own works and up the slope to the scene of the explosion, where they found a large and deep crater. Meantime the Confederate on each side brought guns to bear on the advancing Federals and their Infantry to fire at them. The Federals took position in the crater, which occupied a considerable space, but they could not get farther. General Beauregard commanded that part of the Confederate line. Mahone's Division was ordered to that position and made its way by a ravine concealed from the enemy. A furious bombardment was going on, the Confederate Batteries to the right and left of the crater formed by the explosion of the mine, replied vigorously. Captain J. H. Chamberlayne's Battery on the right and Colonel H. P. Jones' Artillery on the left took a very active part. The latter had wisely arranged his guns for just such an event, for the Confederates suspected that the enemy were preparing a mine in that locality. Mahone's Division was deployed on Blandford Hill and advanced against the enemy, whose lines were about to move

forward, drove them back and forced all who remained, into the crater.
A bloody hand to hand conflict took place. In a short time those who
remained in the crater surrendered and were sent to the rear, many of
them were negro soldiers, some from our city of Norfolk. Many of our
old Regiment, the 6th Virginia, were killed or wounded. Lieut. Col.
Williamson lost an arm, Ensign Howard Wright was killed, Sergeant
Whitehurst, of Portsmouth, acted very bravely, in fact, there were many
acts of individual heroism. Lieut. Col. Stuart, of the 61st, was present
and has written a graphic account. I was near the scene, but was not
called upon to participate. I saw the negro prisoners going to the rear.
The next day was quiet. Captain Richard Walke and I were lying in
our tent at night talking, when I felt something like a grasshopper. We
got up and shook the top blanket, then laid down. As I stretched out,
I felt something like the prick of a needle in my left foot. I got up,
put on my boots, and went to the kitchen fire, called my servant, who
lighted a candle, it was then midnight, went and examined the blanket where Walke was still lying. We found a Moccasin snake coiled up.
Walke got up rapidly and the snake was killed, but I had been bitten.
A Surgeon was sent for and remedies applied, my servant willingly
sucked the wound. A pint of new apple brandy was procured with difficulty, and later Lieut. Col. Cutts sent a pint of peach brandy, which
he had just received from his home in Georgia. All of which I consumed in order to counteract the effect of the poison. The Surgeon
arrived in about two hours. I was very sick and unconscious, but next
morning was much better, although the foot was very much swollen. A
sick leave of absence was procured, and with my servant, I left for the
home of Mrs. Chamberlaine's father, Mr. Dillard at Rocky Mount, Va.
We arrived there on the third day, not without difficulty, for the railroad had been cut and bridges burned by raiders, a manner of warfare
taught the enemy by our great Cavalry leader, General J. E. B. Stuart. I
am greatly indebted to an old lady named Ashenhurst, who lived near
Rocky Mount, for a reasonably speedy cure of the bite. She secured
in the forest some snake weed, made a poultice of the leaves, and also
some tea to take internally. At the end of a month the swelling was
reduced, but there were some yellowish streaks up to my knee. I returned to the Army about September 1st and found Walke occupying
the same resting place. Surgeon H. M. Nash had reported and we three

lived together awhile, when Col. Walker's Headquarters were moved to a point near the Old Fair Grounds and in rear of Battery No. 45. General A. P. Hill's Headquarters were quite near. Colonel Walker was promoted to Brigadier of Artillery. While we were there Captain Thos. A. Brander was married to a daughter of the Rev. Lewis Walke, a cousin of Captain Richard Walke, who procured a leave and acted as one of the groomsmen.

While I was off on sick leave the news received from the North led us to believe that the Northern people were anxious to make peace, but a month or two later an entire change of sentiment seemed to have taken place. The Presidential Campaign was then in progress. Lincoln had been re-nominated by the Republicans and McClellan by the Democratic Party. General A. P. Hill and Mrs. Hill dined one day with General and Mrs. Walker, and in the course of the conversation I heard General Hill say that he hoped McClellan would be elected, because if it became necessary to surrender, he would prefer to do so to McClellan. He and McClellan had been close friends; at the marriage of the latter, Hill had acted as groomsman.

The siege of Petersburg was long and wearisome, it lasted nine months. At times there was great activity on parts of the long line which extended from five miles south of Petersburg to eight miles east of Richmond, at least thirty miles. The Otey Battery had joined our Corps and I met my friend, John H. Sharp, occasionally, who was detailed as a courier attached to the Headquarters of General E. P. Alexander, Chief of Artillery of the 1st Corps. General Longstreet had almost recovered from his wound, and was welcomed back to the Army. General Beauregard had been ordered South and General R. H. Anderson succeeded to his Command. Col. D. A. Weisiger was promoted to Brigadier General and retained Command of Mahone's old Brigade. There were also many promotions in the Artillery. Wm. Pegram was promoted to Colonel, D. G. McIntosh to Colonel, Thos. A. Brander to Major, Poague to Lieut. Colonel, Jos. McGraw to Major. Towards the end of the year General Walker was indisposed and appealed for a sick leave. He asked me to take it by the regular channel for approval. I rode to General Lee's Headquarters just before sunset. He occupied Pryor's house in Petersburg. One entered the front door and on the right was General Lee's room, and the left Lieut. Col. W. H. Taylor's office. I went in the latter and Col. Taylor was attending to the application when General Lee entered. I rose and saluted and the General said, "Good morning, sir." It was then late in the afternoon and his remark made me feel a great desire to leave, so, as soon as Col. Taylor handed me the application, which had the approval written on it, I left. The old General was probably fatigued by the great responsibility of his position. Supplies were scarce and there were a great many desertions from the ranks. No doubt he knew that the lines were closing around his Army and that he saw that disaster was approaching.

It was now winter, not much going on at the front, and it was usual for officers to have their wives come to Petersburg and find a boarding house in that city. It was, however, hard to find suitable places. Captain George C. Reid, a Quartermaster, was stationed there and had rented a house on Halifax Street. His family had been neighbors of my father in Norfolk, Va., so he invited me to take a spare room in his house, which I accepted with thanks. He had with him his wife and two young daughters, Alice and Annie. Mrs. Chamberlaine arrived with her father and was duly installed with the Reids. As provisions were scarce my rations were turned over to them daily. It was a great favor on the part of the Reids and I have always felt exceedingly grateful to them. Mrs. Chamberlaine remained there six weeks. Cannon and mortar firing was going on continually and we could from that house hear the explosions and also the crack of the rifles of the pickets, who kept up a continual battle.

Mr. Dillard was very anxious to see the works and the enemy's lines, so I ordered my horse and a spare one to be taken to Jarratt's Hotel and we rode to the front. Our horses were so much reduced by the lack of forage that he was astonished at their condition, and said if I would send my black mare up to Rocky Mount he would put her in the pasture to fatten up and let me have another. When Mrs. Chamberlaine was ready to return, I obtained a short leave and accompanied her home, and sent the mare by railroad. On my return I rode the new horse to Lynchburg, sixty-two miles. When I reached a point five miles from that city, there was a steep hill to ascend, and I dismounted and walked beside the horse. He was tricky and as we reached the top of the hill, jumped away out of my reach, turned around and ran away. I tried to catch him, but when I got almost to him, he trotted off again;

that was at the top of the hill, back towards his old home. I met a carriage with one lady, a colored man was driving. The lady refused my request to allow her servant to assist me to catch my horse, and drove on in the direction my horse had gone. I was almost in despair, for I thought he would certainly return the fifty-seven miles to Rocky Mount. I sat down on the side of the road, and had not to wait very long, for soon the lady's servant came back riding my horse, some distance back on the road they had found him grazing. With a gratified heart I rewarded the servant, mounted and was soon at Lynchburg. The day had been beautiful and no other contretemps had occurred on that long ride. I had sent my servant by the railroad from Big Lick to Lynchburg, and he met me there. It was easy to get transportation from Petersburg, but not on freight trains going towards the Army, because the cars were all needed for supplies for the Army. I stayed that night in Lynchburg with my good friend, John R. Todd, he being employed in the Nitre and Mining Bureau and had a comfortable place on the Island, near the railroad depot. He was very kind and hospitable to me, and to many other friends. A snow storm came up that night and the next morning the ground had a covering of six inches of snow. I sent my servant on the horse to Petersburg, one hundred and twenty-five miles. It took him nearly a week to make the trip. I left by the train that afternoon, but the snow was so deep in the railroad cuts that it stalled before we had gone twenty-five miles. The passengers had to remain on that train all night and all of the next day, when we had gotten as far as Pamplin's Depot; then one night there. The weather was milder the third day, and our train reached Petersburg in the afternoon. The first news we heard was, that there had been a battle near Burgess' Mill on our right flank and General John C. Pegram had been killed. Military operations had now become more active. It was about the first of March. The number of desertions had increased. Our line was so long that it was more like a skirmish line than a line of battle. The latter part of March, General Lee determined to strike a blow and assembled a force of Infantry and Cavalry near Blanford Church. We were ordered to arms at daylight all along the line. The force under General Gordon rushed forward and captured a considerable part of the enemy's line a little to the left of the crater; but was not able to hold it long, for the enemy rushed reinforcements to the scene, and Gordon's force was obliged to return to our lines. In the afternoon I was sent to notify Major Richardson that Captain Grandy's Battery would be relieved that night. There was a sort of truce then on that part of the line, the enemy did not fire at everything that appeared. I went by the covered way to the Battery, saw Major Richardson and he called my attention to a movement of Federal troops on their Military Railroad towards their left. He took me to the crest of the earthworks, from which point I could see the movement, which I reported on my return. A little while before that it would have been certain destruction to go on the breastworks, but our neighbors were then more pacifically disposed. That night I went again to that Battery to see it withdrawn and conduct it a part of the way to its new position, which was several miles to the right. It was withdrawn about one hour before daylight. Several weeks before that, Captain Charles R. Grandy and I rode over to see the crater. We examined it carefully, it was like an excavation, long and comparatively narrow, our line had been established directly after the battle in rear of the place, and the rains had washed the sides, giving the appearance of a railroad cut. The clay taken from the bottom was found to be of an excellent quality for pipes. On the 31st of March a large force of the enemy had been collected on our extreme right, a number of our Batteries had been sent there. On that morning, while there, quite a brisk engagement took place and we saw Wise's Brigade with others charge the 5th Corps of the Federal Army, which was driven back some distance.

That evening, after I returned to our quarters, I remarked to a friend, that our line from the dam in front of Battery 45 to Burgess' Mill did not appear to me any stronger than a horsehair. We did not have the troops to make it any stronger. About this time General Walker was directed to organize two Companies for temporary Infantry duty from the supernumerary Artillerymen. Those men were ordered to appear at our Headquarters one morning and were duly organized into two Companies of about sixty men each, and the Non-Commissioned officers appointed pro tem. They were armed and equipped as Infantry and sent to man Fort Gregg, which was a small earthwork raised about two hundred yards in rear of the main line, with its front perpendicular to the latter, and located about three hundred yards from Battery 45. There was another work two hundreds yards farther back from the main line. In case of a flanking movement by the enemy those earthworks were intended to be occupied by troops to repel it.

By daylight on April 2nd heavy firing being heard on our left, General Walker mounted his horse and rode rapidly in that direction, followed by Captain Walke and myself. He found the enemy had captured a small portion of our line near the Reeve's Salient. As he saw me approach, he directed me to go to the line in front of Fort Gregg and bring him a section of Artillery which was posted there. I started at once, but when I reached Fort Gregg, I was informed that the main line in front had been seized by the enemy and the section of rifle guns with it, together with other pieces, and that Lieut. Ellet had been killed. Captain J. Ham Chamberlayne was there, and was in great distress because his friend Ellet had been killed and the guns captured. I started back to inform General Walker and met him half way. He went at once to that point, where Ellet had been killed. It appeared that the main force of the enemy had left and the captured line with the guns was held by a skirmish line only. A few of our Infantry men were standing around and accompanied by General Walker, they drove the enemy away and recovered several of the captured guns. Very soon afterwards we saw a Brigade of Infantry, commanded by General Harris of Mississippi, coming from Petersburg, about four hundred strong. At the same time, a column of Federals marched by file over our line of works about one mile to the south of where we were standing. As soon as that column had passed over our entrenchment, it faced to the right and advanced in line of battle towards us. The Brigade of General Harris deployed in line advanced to meet them. The Federals outnumbered them by one thousand at least. Both lines were advancing, and when within musket range, a few shots were exchanged. Then Harris' Brigade retired slowly, and when it reached Fort Gregg, a part of it entered that Fort, thus reinforcing the force of Artillerymen armed as Infantry, and the other part occupied Fort Whitworth, about two hundred yards to the right. There were also some men of Lane's Brigade which had been driven from our main line, who entered Fort Gregg, besides a section of rifle guns of the Washington Artillery, commanded by Lieut. McElroy.

The enemy's line halted and its Commander made preparations for an assault. General Walker with his staff went to Battery No. 45, from which point there was a good view of the two Forts and the terrain in front. A small stream flows between Battery No. 45 and Fort Gregg, and winds along the valley in front of the Confederate works and empties its waters into the Appomattox River above Petersburg. The limbers of the section of the Washington Artillery had been sent back to that stream. Seeing the preparations for the assault of that Fort, General Walker directed me to go and say to the Commander of the Artillery that he thought two guns should be withdrawn. I started and found Lieut. Col. Eschleman at the stream near the limbers, and delivered the message. He was the Commander of the Battalion of Washington Artillery. But there was not time enough to send the limbers with the horses to the Fort and withdraw the guns before the first assault. Immediately afterwards the enemy delivered an assault and was repulsed, but remained close to the Fort and kept up a fusillade.

I had returned to the hill where General Walker was watching the action. He had sent Captain Walke with a similar message to Fort Whitworth and two guns were withdrawn from that work, the enemy had not shown any disposition to assault it. Very soon the enemy made another assault on Fort Gregg. There were some of the soldiers' cabins in front of Fort Whitworth occupied during the winter, and our men set fire to them, and they were burning furiously while the enemy was occupied at Fort Gregg. The second assault was also repulsed.

In a short time a third assault was made, and succeeded, the Federal soldiers climbed the slope of the work on its right flank and filed along the crest and fired on the Confederates huddled together on the parade. We could see them very plainly. A color bearer ran out of the Fort with his flag; two men pursued him, but he passed the little stream. Men near Battery No. 45 fired at his pursuers and they went back to Fort Gregg. So the color bearer escaped with his flag. Major General C. M. Wilcox was in command of that part of the Confederate line, and was standing near the limbers of the guns of the Washington Artillery just in rear of Fort Gregg, by the little stream. We witnessed the whole of that battle at Fort Gregg and felt very indignant when we saw the Federal troops fire down on its brave defenders after they had crowned the ramparts. There is no doubt that our men were sacrificed, but the intention was to hold the Federal troops in check until reinforcements could arrive and the inner line of works surrounding

Petersburg be manned. That result was accomplished, for Longstreet's troops from Richmond arrived about that time on the scene, and the inner line of works, a very strong position, was occupied by them. Our line then commenced at the Appomattox River below the city and stretched around Petersburg and rested on the same river above the city, and was firmly held until night. General A. P. Hill had been killed early in the morning in attempting to reach that part of his Corps on the right which had been cut off by the Federal troops, who had broken through the line to the southwest of Battery Gregg. He was shot by a Federal skirmisher. General A. P. Hill was regarded as one of the best of the Corps Commanders. He was very much esteemed by his men, and was a dashing soldier, and beloved by his officers.

Chapter 18

End Approaches

No attempt was made by the enemy to force the new line, and at sunset it remained as when established in the forenoon. General Walker went to Field Headquarters, where General Lee was sitting on the porch of a dwelling with General Longstreet. Hill's Corps was placed under the command of the latter. The order was given to evacuate the lines at dusk. I was sent to withdraw the Artillery of the 3rd Corps posted on the line to the left of Battery No. 45, and Captain Walke to withdraw that on the right of that position. All of the guns of the 3rd Corps were promptly withdrawn and marched quietly through the city to Campbell's Bridge and after crossing the river, proceeded on the Hickory Road towards the Clover Coal Mine. Very little rest was obtained that night. We were moving when the day dawned on April 3rd. There were many refugees from the city of Petersburg. I saw the Reverend George D. Armstrong plodding along the road on foot. He was pastor of the Presbyterian Church in Norfolk and it was reported had been harshly treated by the Federal Officer in Command of that city and finally expelled from the Federal lines, and had been in Petersburg for several weeks, but was now compelled to move again, when that city was evacuated. As he was then an old man and seemed to be without anything to protect him from rain or the dampness of the earth, I presented him with a rubber blanket which I had secured during the battle of Chancellorsville, for which he seemed to be very grateful. The retreat continued until the morning of the 5th, when, after having crossed the Appomattox River again, we arrived at Amelia Court House, where Sheridan's Cavalry was found barring the road to Danville, and the railroad supply trains had been sent back towards Lynchburg. As those trains contained food for the Army, there was great disappointment, for the troops had consumed all they had taken with them from the lines at Petersburg.

While at Amelia Court House, I witnessed the destruction of a number of caissons filled with ammunition, but never learned whether it was an accident, or by design. General Lee ordered a few Battalions of Artillery—those best equipped—to accompany the Infantry and ordered all the rest to be formed into a column under the Command of General R. L. Walker, and proceed through Buckingham County towards Lynchburg. The Artillery column left the main column at Deatonsville, crossed the Appomattox River, and took the route as directed. On the way to Deatonsville we saw several places where the enemy's Cavalry had attacked the wagon train and burned some of the wagons, so after crossing the river, Captain Walke was ordered to have the bridge burned, which duty was performed. The column proceeded some miles and at dark bivouacked for the night. Our force consisted of a part of the Artillery of each Corps, with two Battalions of dismounted Artillery armed as Infantry, all accompanied by their wagons.

Next day we passed through Cumberland and Buckingham Counties, and on the 7th of April arrived at a place called New Store, where the road we were moving on comes into that over which the main body of the Army was marching, and about eleven miles northwest of Farmville. Here we observed certain indications of a rout; some teams with harness, but no wagons. Food was very scarce, but we managed to collect a little on the way. Our column continued its march, and at dusk bivouacked. The moon was about full and the weather clear. The column was ordered to move forward at one o'clock A. M. Major H. M. Nash, Chief Surgeon of the Artillery of the 3rd Corps, accompanied the General and his staff. That night he, Captain Walke, and myself, were discussing the situation and as there was a strong probability of losing some of the wagons, we determined to put on as many of our clothes as we could wear, the weather was cool and the extra clothing was not uncomfortable.

Major R. C. Taylor, of Norfolk, Virginia, joined us that afternoon and when we halted for the night, he heard from some one passing, that his brother, Lieut. Col. Walter H. Taylor, had been killed on the retreat. He therefore determined to turn back to meet the main body of the Army, which was coming on the road several miles behind our column. The report was not true.

We moved at one A. M. and passed through Appomattox Court House about midday and two miles west of the Court House took a road to the left, which led to Appomattox Station on the Southside Railroad. When within one-third of a mile of that depot, we found a large open field. It was then nearly two o'clock and General Walker ordered the column to halt and form a park, so the men could eat their food, as well as the horses. General W. N. Pendleton rode up and entered into conversation with General Walker, in the course of which he directed that the number of guns should be reduced to the point that could be drawn by the number of horses in suitable condition—many horses being completely worn out—to fill up ammunition chests and to bury such guns as could not be drawn. I was sent with that message to Colonel W. L. Cabell, whose command was a few hundred feet away. As I was delivering the message, the advance guard of Custer's Division of Federal Cavalry rode up and commenced firing their revolvers.

Chapter 19

Last Battle

As soon as the park was formed, I had gone on to the railroad station, and seeing Surgeon James D. Gait, he told me that it was reported there, that the Federal Cavalry had reached Pamplin's Depot, ten miles east, and would probably reach Appomattox by nine P.M. I returned at once to General Walker and reported what I had heard, and was sent at once to Colonel Cabell with the message. The Federal Cavalry was much nearer to us than the report indicated. General Walker directed me to ride back to the Lynchburg Road to get any troops that I might find, to come to our support. I met one of our Battallions armed as Infantry, led by Captain Walke, advancing in line of battle towards the enemy. Not finding on the Lynchburg road anything but a few stragglers, I returned to the front. General Walker directed the wagon train to retire by the Lynchburg road.

As many guns as could be brought into action commenced firing at the approaching Cavalry, the Battalions armed as Infantry joined in the battle and held the enemy back, but they seized the trains of cars standing at the depot. About one hour after the first attack, Gary's Brigade of Cavalry, several hundred strong, arrived, and having dismounted took position on the right of the line. General Pendleton took position a little in rear of the line and I remained with him. Our men stood off the enemy until dusk, repelling numerous attacks, until the greater part of the guns and wagons had moved off towards Lynchburg, when nearly the whole of Custer's Division having arrived, they made a charge and swept over all that was left, some twenty guns and a few wagons (among the latter our Headquarter's wagon), which were captured.

A section of the Washington Artillery brought up our rear and held the enemy back from our line of retreat, holding a position at the junc-

tion of the road to the depot and the road to Lynchburg. We had a
number of men killed, wounded and some taken prisoners. Our Commissary, Major A. W. Parker, lost an arm and was sent in an ambulance
to Lynchburg. He had taken a musket and fought in the ranks. Major
Miller was with the section of the Washington Artillery.

After riding about one mile on the Lynchburg Road, I came up
with General Walker and the rest of his Staff. He directed me to return
and bring off the section of the Washington Artillery. I went back at
once; we did not know what had happened during that charge and I
supposed those two guns had been captured with the rest. Neverthe-
less, it was the General's duty to send after the rear guard and mine to
go for it, but on arriving at the position it had held so firmly, I found
it still ready for anything which might turn up. The enemy held in
check by those two guns, had stopped and taken the road on which
our main body was approaching.

Our Surgeon, Major H. M. Nash, had been caught in the charge of
the Federal Cavalry; had been thrown from his horse, and dragged by
one foot in the stirrup quite a long distance; his foot then was disen-
gaged and he rolled himself to the ditch on the side of the road, thus
escaping being injured by the hoofs of horses following. He told me
afterwards that his extra clothing helped to keep his body from being
bruised. He was found and kindly treated by a Federal Surgeon and
recovered his horse. He lived until 1911, a distinguished surgeon and
physician in Norfolk, highly esteemed and beloved.

I gave the order to the section of Artillery to limber up and led
them to the column, but it was nearly daylight, before we caught up
with it. Soon after daylight appeared, Surgeon Carrington arrived at
our bivouac and gave the following message from General R. E. Lee:
"I intend to try to cut my way out at daybreak. If you can reach us
and think you can be of any service, do so. If not disband your Command and allow the men to go either to join General Jos. E. Johnson
in North Carolina or to their homes, as they may elect."

Our column was at least ten miles from the main body, and when
the message was received, it was then past the hour for the attack. General Walker decided to disband the command, which was done. Many
of the guns were dismantled, wheels cut and guns buried. The General and Staff took a road leading to Bent Creek Ford on the James

River; before reaching the ford we met some of our Cavalrymen, who said the Army of Northern Virginia was then being surrendered. Captain Walke decided to go back to surrender, but afterwards changed his plan, and went to join the Army of General Jos. E. Johnson. We crossed at the ford, the river was high, and the water came over my boot tops. Proceeding along the tow path, we reached the Estate of Doctor Gilmer near Tye River Warehouse, about 8:00 P. M. Mrs. Gilmer was a sister of the General. Doctor Gilmer's brother was there, he had served in the Legislature with Mr. Hughes Dillard, Mrs. Chamberlaine's father, and on learning that I intended to make my way to the latter's home, he sent this message, "What do you think now of the rights of the States in the Territories?"

Next morning the members of the Staff separated. The General remained. I went as far as North Garden, where I stopped one night at Mr. Slaughter's, whose home was near Cedar Mountain, in Culpepper County, but had taken refuge at a place at North Garden. Next day I crossed the Blue Ridge Mountains alone at Rock Fish Gap, and arrived at Waynesboro at sunset. There was a report in that town that General Lee had surrendered, but a kind blacksmith put a shoe on my horse and took Confederate money in payment. A gentleman named Turk took me home with him, where I spent that night, for which I was very grateful. He gave me an early breakfast and directed me to Tinkling Spring, where I found the main road to Lexington. I stayed that night at Wallace's Inn, I think in the town of Brownsburg. Next morning I passed through Lexington and went as far as Colonel Poague's farm. Col. Poague was one of our most distinguished Artillery Officers. We had been very good friends in the Army and he was very hospitable. I have invited him to my home, but he never got as far as Norfolk, but did serve a term in the Legislature.

From his house, I rode to Big Lick, now called Roanoke, forty-seven miles. As I passed through the town of Buchanan, the churches were open and services being held. We had decided that it would be best to leave our sabers at the Gilmer's, as we might meet some of the enemy's troops, and be conducted to prison. As I approached Big Lick, I decided to avoid it, if occupied by the enemy. I reconnoitered and found it was not, so went to Trout's Inn and spent the night. Mr. Trout kindly accepted a five-dollar Confederate note for my bill. I presume the news of Lee's surrender had been received in the village, but he did not object to the money. Next day I reached the residence of Mr. Dillard by twelve o'clock noon, twenty-eight miles. Of course I was warmly welcomed by all. They had had no news from me since the retreat commenced.

I am nearly at the end of my story, but it was necessary to surrender and get a parole before my connection with the Military service would be completely severed. I remained at Mr. Dillard's home in the village of Rocky Mount about five weeks. While sitting on the front porch one morning a troop of Federal Cavalry rode through the town. They were in search of General J. A. Early. They did not find him, for he had notice and had taken refuge at the home of Captain Woods, twelve miles away. The troop stopped at the house of Mr. John Saunders, Sheriff of the County, about one mile from the village. I started to go there, but it came on to rain, and I concluded to wait for a better opportunity to surrender.

While there, we heard of the assassination of the President of the United States and were very sorry that such an act had been committed by one pretending to be in sympathy with the South.

Chapter 20

Return

About the first of June, in company with Mr. Dillard, I rode to Danville, the 6th Corps of the Federal Army was stationed there. When we arrived at Martinsville, the County seat of Henry, we rode into a company of Federal Infantry. I was not noticed and after a short conversation between Mr. Dillard and the officers in command, we started for Fairmount, the Estate of Mr. Dillard's mother, who was then living.

After a visit of a day or two, we started for Danville. We found that town full of troops. There was at that time much talk about sending the Federal Army to Mexico, to drive away the French troops, Napoleon III having established Maximillian on the throne of Mexico and was supporting him by a Corps of French troops under Marshall Bazine.

But the United States authorities, in order to keep the Southern States in subjection, stationed a Company of Infantry or Cavalry in each County.

I applied for a parole at the office of the Provost Marshall, which was given without hesitation. This permitted me to return to my home and to remain undisturbed so long as I obeyed the laws of the Country. I left on the Richmond train the next morning, arrived at Richmond at midnight. The clerk at the Spottswood Hotel said he was not allowed to receive Confederate Soldiers, but he permitted me to stay in the front window the rest of the night, also two other Confederates: one was an officer of the Confederate States' Marines, and the other Captain William Face, a pilot who had lived in Norfolk. At least we had a roof over our heads. We left at dawn of day for the Norfolk steamboat landing. In the afternoon I arrived at my native city after an absence of a little more than three years.

The retreat from Petersburg was very hard on the Army of Northern Virginia. Its numbers had been reduced by casualties, provisions were scarce and by the end of the 6th day General Lee had reached the conclusion that it was impossible to keep up the struggle any longer and wisely decided to seek an agreement with General U. S. Grant for a cessation of hostilities. The latter replied that he had no authority to do anything more than to accept a surrender, but his terms were very liberal. He allowed both officers and men to keep their horses and issued rations to our almost famished troops. On the day before the surrender by General Lee had our column of Reserve Artillery not stopped where it did, but gone beyond the Southside Railroad, leaving a small detachment to procure supplies from the railroad trains, which were only one-quarter of a mile from the place where we had halted, it seems probable that it would have escaped the Federal Cavalry and reached Danville. But we had no information of the movements of the Federal Cavalry and supposed they were following the main body of our Army, which was some twenty miles behind us. But the result would have been the same. The Armies of the Confederate States were about worn out and could hold together but a little while longer. The Southern States lost a great many men and much treasure, but those who survived the War had learned a great deal by their experience and many whose health had been feeble had become strong by the out-of-door life, all of which was necessary, for most of them had really to begin life again, and the Army had maintained its honor.

General Remarks

The majority of the people of Virginia was not in favor of a resort to arms to settle the question in dispute between the Sections: they preferred Peace in the Union and many efforts were made by our Statesmen to prevent conflict, but the radicals on both sides were so insistent on their respective views that all such efforts were futile.

Once War declared, then it was not only the duty but the desire of all the young men of my acquaintance to do their best to maintain the position of the Confederate States. As to the martial qualities of the men of the two sections, those of the South seemed to have a little more *élan* than the natives of the North, while the latter possessed more persistence. Both were brave, hence the terrible battles and the fearful slaughter which took place during the ensuing four years. The benefits of an education at the West Point Military Academy was shared by both sides. Any man who had been educated at that Institution was eagerly sought after in the South to fill a prominent place in the Army, and the men in the ranks, as well as the young officers, had great confidence in their ability to lead them properly.

Ex-Governor William Smith was appointed Colonel of the 49th Virginia Infantry, which regiment at one time was attached to the Brigade of General William Mahone. I do not think the Governor pretended to have a military education, but he was a brave man, and like a good planter was careful of those in his charge: two very important qualities for a commanding officer, and when he wished his skirmishers to advance and said to them "Sic em, boys," they understood as well what was required of them as if he had given the Command as provided in the books on Military Tactics. Then he was an elderly man, and when on the march in a hot sun did not disdain the use of an umbrella, which action some military men would have condemned. Governor Smith reached the rank of Major-General before the close of the war.

The troops stationed around Norfolk, Va., under Major-General Benj. Huger, although near the enemy were not brought into actual contact until they participated in the battles near Richmond, Va. Just before those battles occurred, an order of General James Longstreet was read to our Regiment at parade, in which occurred this language: "While the noise of battle is indeed terrifying and seems to threaten universal destruction, after all but few soldiers are actually slain." I well remember hearing that order read and it had a good effect on the soldiers who had not been under fire in a general engagement. It was felt by them that General Longstreet knew all about it, and there was a good chance for them to go through all that fearful firing and come out without a scratch or perhaps with only a slight wound. After the seven days' battles were fought and we had an opportunity to read the lists of killed and wounded, we felt that the General had treated the subject lightly, but then we had been through it and became, as it were, seasoned.

The most unfortunate thing about the battles fought early in the war was the impetuosity and lack of experience of the high ranking officers. Many attacks were made by single Brigades and even single Regiments, which were quickly repulsed with great loss, while if the whole front line could have moved at the same moment, a different result would probably have followed. That was perhaps due to two or more reasons; first: Some officers wished to have the credit of capturing guns; second: The orders to advance were not explicit; third: Lack of Staff Officers to communicate orders and information. Such things happen to the Army making an attack. On the other side, the party attacked should be always ready to receive the attacking foe. I believe the great loss sustained by the Confederates, in the battles around Richmond, Va., was due to those causes. As time passed the General Officers became more proficient and their men became veterans.

To supply the army with food seemed in those days to be a very difficult thing. I am sure the Army of Northern Virginia never reached to the 100,000 mark, and I have since often thought how our large cities, even those in Virginia, always seem to have abundant supplies for their inhabitants, and I have asked myself the question, did we formerly receive a large part of the supplies for the Southern States from North of Mason and Dixon's line. Vegetables were scarce, the Confederate Soldiers lived on flour and corn meal and bacon or beef most of the time the war lasted. At one time there was a ration of plug tobacco issued. I used smoking tobacco but had no use for the plug, so gave it away. Officers were allowed two rations each day, one for himself and the other for his servant, and forage for two horses, if he had two.

There were many highly intelligent men who served as couriers attached to the Headquarters of General Officers. The duties of these men differed but little from those of aides-de-camp, who were regularly commissioned officers, and deserved to be rewarded in the same degree as the commissioned staff, but the law restricted the number of those who received commissions. Some General Officers acknowledged the services of their couriers in their official reports, but the practice was not generally followed. Many of them received commissions later in the War. While our Company "G," 6th Virginia Infantry, formed a part of the garrison at Craney Island, only four miles from our homes, many little tricks were resorted to by the men to go off without leave and spend a night at home. On one occasion when the steamboat was about to leave the wharf in the afternoon, I was standing on the wharf, I saw the wife of one of our men standing at a window of the saloon, apparently very sad at leaving, the yellow shade of the next window was lowered, but the western sun cast the shadow of her husband full upon the yellow shade and I recognized it distinctly. His person was concealed, but the shadow told on him. In such cases it was best not to notice the little trick, so I let it pass. The volunteers were making a great sacrifice for their country and I did not think we ought to be too strict in little matters. I had seen only his shadow and not the man. His absence was not officially reported to me. For shelter at that post log huts were built; a detail was sent to the neighboring pine forest, and cut poles; these were used to build the huts and were duly chinked and the openings closed with mud, making quite comfortable quarters during the cold weather. When Norfolk was evacuated the garrison of Craney Island marched to Suffolk, twenty-five miles distant, and then proceeded by railroad to Petersburg.

The following list contains the names of the members of Company "G," 6th Virginia Infantry, not heretofore mentioned in these memoirs:

Catlett, John R.
Styron, Oscar M.
Archer, R. L.
Baylor, Robt. B.
Bell, Robert S.
Clark, Fred. W.
Deiches, W.
Fentress, Thomas
Fletcher, Oliver N.
Goodridge, T. E.
Hopkins, Richard
Langhorn, Wm. W.
Merritt, John B.
McKenny, Wm. W.
Reid, J. T. S.
Robinson, W. C.
Rosenberg, M.
Seal, John R.
Butt, J. L. D.
Biggs, Wm. G.
Biggs, James H.
Chisman, John R.
Core, John H.
Gordon, John D.
Gordon, W. R.
Holmes, Alex. T.
Kerr, Edward.
Monsden, B. A.
McPhail, C. H.
Phentz, Geo. M.
Robertson, C.
Robins, Geo. S.
Rowland, J. H.

Smith, J. K.
Shipp, John S.
Southgate, L.
Segar, John
Smith, Henry
Stone, David S.
Voss, Albert C.
Williams, John N.
Walsh, William
Simmons, Albert B.
Hill, John T.
Arrington, Peter
Bell, Douglass
Bell, James N.
Cole, Cornelius M.
Dey, James B.
Fitchett, Julius M.
Freeman, Robert
Goodridge, Geo. K.
Hardy, Thos. A.
Lawson, A. S.
Moore, Walter S.
Murray, John
Reynolds, H. S.
Robinson, William
Rowe, S. D.
Seal, Wm. B.
Segar, A. S.
Smoot, William
Thomas, Rich. S.
Ward, Josiah J.
Wise, W. M. B.
Young, Thos. A.

Umstadter, M.

Whiting, W. N.

Wicker, D. H. C.

Marsden, J. B.

Stokes, M. N.

Beale, Brook

Cason, Benj. F.

Greyot, R. S.

Hudgins, W. R.

Keeling, S. S.

Morris, J. S.

Saunders, Palmer

Taylor, Robertson

Wilkinson, H. D.

Collier, James M.

Freeman, Joseph N.

Gwynn, T. P.

Hyman, T. M.

Mapp, R. A.

Mallory, Chas. O.

Stone, Geo. F.

Walker, Geo. B.

Walker, J. T.

Cannon, D. C.

Foeman, C. W.

Hunter, W. W.

Jaquineau, A. H.

Milhado, A. G.

Portlock, R. G.

Tunstall, Alex.

Langley, W. H.

Of the above many were appointed to important positions in the Army, some were transferred to other Commands and some discharged for disability.

Index